TRUE COURAGE

"I have no strength to hold up, to hope, to live. But in my ears there still echo the last words of my mother. 'Carry on, do not despair, for your mother's sake!' Only these words keep the spark of life aglow within me."

—Janina Heshele, Poland

FACING REALITY

"Mum had gone into the kitchen when the shooting began. We could hear the bullets whizzing over the house and ricocheting off the corrugated iron on the factory wall behind our house. The bullets smashed through the kitchen window."

—Margaret McCrory, Northern Ireland

INNERMOST SECRETS

"I'm carrying a deep wound, a wound that keeps getting deeper and deeper every time peace is postponed and manipulated."

—Ghareeb, the West Bank

WHY DO THEY

Young Lives C...............ct

Contents

THE HOLOCAUST AND WORLD WAR II

Introduction   5
Janine Phillips, Poland   9
Dirk Van der Heide, Holland   29
Janina Heshele, Poland   50
Helga Kinsky-Pollack, Austria   56
Mary Berg, Poland   61
Ina Konstantinova, Russia   88
Colin Perry, England   100

"THE TROUBLES" IN NORTHERN IRELAND

Introduction   133
"Eamon," John McConnell   141
"Internment," Margaret McCrory   147
"Kneecapped," Margaret E. Simpson   153
"Clutch of Fear," P. J. Quinn   156
"Condemned," Brenda Murphy   171
"The Leaving of Liverpool," Kevin Byers   190

"Unwelcome Callers," Alison Östnas   196

"Neil," Lisa Burrows   200

"The Road Rats Cometh," Stephen Hoey   207

THE ISRAELI/PALESTINIAN CONFLICT

Introduction   213

"Going to Jerusalem," Gunter David   217

"A Christian Palestinian's Story," Wadad Saba   229

"Marked for Destruction," Ibtisam S. Barakat   238

"Born in Bethlehem," Marina N. Riadi   249

"*Alti Zachen*," Victoria Kay-Feinerman   259

"A Look into Memory," Ghareeb (pseudonym) 264

"Face of Peace," Redrose (pseudonym)   267

"My Life on the Firing Line," Racheli Tal 275

"Two Awful Weeks in March," Liran Zvibel   286

Credits   291

About the Author   295

THE

HOLOCAUST

AND

WORLD WAR II

EUROPE
IN 1942

Helsinki
St. Petersburg
Stockholm
Tallinn
ESTONIA
Kashin
6
Riga
Moscow
LATVIA
Baltic
Sea
RUSSIA
LITHUANIA
Kovno
Danzig
16
Vilna
Minsk
POLAND
Bialisk
CHELMNO
TREBLINKA
1
Lodz
5
Warsaw
SOBIBOR
Kielce
15
Kiev
BELZEC
UKRAINE
Cracow
Lvov
3
AUSCHWITZ
E. GALITIA
SLOVAKIA
HUNGARY
Budapest
Nagyvarad
ROMANIA
Bucharest
CROATIA
Belgrade
Sarajevo
SERBIA
MONTE-NEGRO
BULGARIA
ALBANIA
Sofiya

Border of Greater
Germany, 1942
▲ Death Camp
△ Concentration Camp

Legend for Camps
1 Vught
2 Natzweiler-Struthof
3 Neuengamme
4 Ravensbruck
5 Sachsenhausen
6 Dora
7 Buchenwald
8 Oederan
9 Flossenbürg
10 Dachau
11 Mühldorf
12 Lenzing
13 Mauthausen
14 Gross Rosen
15 Maidanek

Introduction

In these excerpts from their secret diaries, young people depict the tremendous suffering that the Nazis caused them and their families during World War II and the Holocaust (1939–1945). Jews and gentiles alike, they describe constant Gestapo harassment, the daily grind of searching for the basic necessities, and the terror of seeing friends and relatives deported to their deaths. Without guarding their feelings or mincing words, they tell us what it was like living every day fearing that it could be their last.

Some of these young writers also wrote about the ways they fought back against their Nazi oppressors, not the least of which was to write what they personally witnessed of their brutality. They wrote with courage—even humor—and they wrote extremely well.

It is astonishing that, even though most of the diaries are as powerful and well-written as Anne Frank's, they have remained obscure while hers has been thought of as *the* child diary of the Holocaust, even though, in some ways, it was not representative of children in the war and the Holocaust. Because Anne Frank was in hiding, she did not experience life in the streets, the ghettos, the concentration camps, as it was lived by millions of children throughout Europe, including those whose diaries appear in this book.

5

To write as frequently and as much as these young people wrote was no simple matter. Pens and paper were difficult to obtain in the concentration camps and ghettos. Those who were under Nazi guard also needed to find a place where they would not be observed writing. And, once they had written their stories, they had to find suitable hiding places for their work so that it would not be confiscated during Gestapo searches. Even for the gentile youth, who lived neither in concentration camps nor in ghettos, writing with bombs falling all around them could not have been easy.

Given these difficulties, why did the children persist in keeping their diaries, in some cases for the entire length of the war? Some say they wrote from loneliness. Separated from their friends and/or family members, they had no one with whom to share what they were going through.

Some of the young people say that they wrote in their diaries as a way of comprehending the horrors with which they were surrounded. Their diaries gave them an opportunity to express their pain and to try to make sense of it. Even if they served no other purpose, the diaries gave the boys and girls the sense that they, as young as they were, had a right to express themselves about what was happening in their world.

With the exception of Colin Perry, who was living in London, these young people were performing private acts of heroism whenever they wrote because, had any of these diaries come to the attention of the Nazis, they could have been shot on the spot. They were speaking out with all their strength against Fascism, and this very outcry may have been the secret to their survival. Those who survived psychologically intact had to believe that what they did on a daily basis could make at least some small difference to someone else. Many of these young writers believed that their diaries would speak for them, after the war was over, and tell the story of the Nazis' "final solution," so that human-kind would not allow such a thing to happen again.

In addition to discernment, wisdom, and depth of reflection, the diarists reveal their resilience and their willingness to extend themselves to others. Despite the Nazi nightmare, they did all they could to rise above their own terror and to ease the suffering of those around them. It is my hope that their courage and in-tegrity will inspire us all to clarify our own values and to fight prejudice and injustice wherever we see it.

In the interest of authenticity, I have not corrected the diarists' punctuation, grammar, and spelling. Nor have I changed the various names they used for geographi-cal locations. These variant place names simply reflect the fact that they lived in different countries and spoke a variety of languages.

Many of the diary entries were undated. When pos-sible, I have deduced dates from the content of the writing and enclosed these dates in brackets.

The ages given for the diarists indicate how old they were when they wrote the first of the entries that I have chosen to excerpt and are not necessarily the ages they were when they began their diaries. The diaries are arranged by age—youngest to oldest.

LAUREL HOLLIDAY
1995

Janine Phillips

10 YEARS OLD

POLAND

*J*anine Phillips began her diary on her tenth birthday, in
May of 1939. She was living in the Polish countryside with
her large, well-to-do family, who had fled Nazi oppression
in nearby Warsaw. Although the family had to accustom
themselves to a simpler way of living, with a certain
amount of ingenuity, they were able to eat three hearty
meals a day, attend Mass every Sunday, and enjoy a certain
number of ordinary pleasures like fishing and celebrations
of feast days.

Nevertheless, they were constantly aware of how pre-
carious their situation was. The family listened to an illegal radio set for every hint of what was happening in the
rest of Europe and in Warsaw. Janine was an avid reporter
of all the news on the domestic as well as the international
fronts. In her diary, she boldly described people's peculi-
arities and peccadillos in such a humorous manner that it
is hard to remember that the family was living in war-torn
Poland and that the reason she had so much time to write
was that it was unsafe for her to go to school. Janine filled
a one-thousand-page notebook the year she was ten.
Then, when she was eleven, she left off diary writing and
returned to school in Warsaw.

In the epilogue to her diary, Janine says that during her
four years in Nazi-occupied Warsaw she attended an illegal school where Polish history and literature were taught.

9

When the Warsaw Ghetto Uprising occurred, she did her "duty" as a Girl Guide and set up a first aid station for the wounded. For this, she was arrested and taken to Germany as a prisoner of war. She was released, in 1945, when she was sixteen, and she continued her education. Janine became a chemist and eventually worked as a researcher for a large company in London. She married and then returned home for a visit in 1965, twenty-one years after she had left Poland.

During this visit, one of her aunts handed her a box containing her childhood diary. Janine translated it into English and it was published, in London, in 1982.

23rd August 1939

Papa says that war is inevitable. I asked Papa why Hitler wants to attack us and Papa said because he's a greedy bully. I only hope he knows that peaceful people don't think him very nice. Grandpa went to see Father Jakob and asked him to say a mass to save us from war. Grandpa remembers many wars and he says that a war not only kills people but it also kills people's souls. That's why Grandpa feels that God ought to intervene, because there won't be many souls left in His Heaven. I quite agree with Grandpa.

1st September 1939

Hitler has invaded Poland. We heard the bad news on the wireless a few minutes before spotting two aeroplanes circling around each other. Just before breakfast, about ten minutes to ten, I was returning from the privy when I heard aeroplanes in the sky. I thought it was manoeuvres. Then I heard some machine-guns and everybody came out from the house to see what was happening. Grandpa said, "My God! It's war!" and rushed indoors to switch on the wireless. The grave news came in a special announcement that German forces have crossed the Polish border and our soldiers are defending our country. Everybody was stunned. With ears glued to the loudspeaker we were trying to catch the fading words. The battery or the accumulator, or both, were packing up. When we could no longer even hear a whisper from the wireless set, Grandpa turned the switch off and looked at our anguished faces. He knelt in front of the picture of Jesus Christ and started to pray aloud. We repeated after Grandpa, "Our Father who art in Heaven, hallowed be Thy name . . ."

Soon after tea, Uncle Tadeusz, my new Aunt Aniela and Papa arrived from Warsaw with some more bad news. Papa said that we were not going back to Warsaw because it was safer to stay here, in the village. He arranged for a wagon to bring our winter clothes and other belongings. I wondered what will happen to our school, but Mama said that when a country is fighting for its survival, there is no time for schooling. All evening Papa has been trying to get the wireless going but did not succeed. Tomorrow, he'll try to get to Warsaw and see what can be done about the set which is so vital to us just now. Please, Dear God, let our brave soldiers beat the nasty Germans.

3rd September 1939

Papa and Mama returned from Warsaw late last night together with our belongings. They hired a horse-drawn wagon and it took them several hours to get here. The roads were packed with soldiers and military vehicles. People in Warsaw are in high spirits and quite ready to fight. I wish I were in Warsaw too, because I can fight quite well when I set my mind to it. Papa brought a new battery, thank goodness, and is fiddling with the wireless at this very moment. Uncle Tadeusz and Aunt Aniela are coming back tomorrow or the day after because Uncle has been making arrangements for someone to mind his shop for him.

Magnificent news! England is going to thrash the Gerries in no time at all. Mr. Chamberlain said that England has declared war against Germany. This welcome news came from the loudspeaker like a blessing from Heaven. I am so glad that we have some good friends abroad. Papa said that Great Britain is a mighty power with a strong Navy and Air Force. Everybody is greatly relieved and we celebrated with a drop of our special vintage wine. I shall have to learn some English because I know only one word, "Goodbye," and that's hardly enough to carry on a conversation with English soldiers. Papa said in three or four weeks they'll be here. When they come, I should like to thank them for helping us to beat Hitler but if I haven't learnt sufficient English to say so, I'll just have to hug them and they'll know what I mean.

4th September 1939

We heard some heavy artillery fire. No-one seems to know where it was coming from. Grandpa took Mama and me to the market to get a stock of food but there was very little we could buy. The farmers are hanging on to their dairy produce and there were very few eggs left, and they have suddenly trebled in price. That also applies to wheat, flour and sugar. Anyway, we've managed to get a few kilogrammes of dry sausage and that will keep for many months. Mama went to see her friends and they sold her a large piece of pork belly and two kilogrammes of dripping. The Jewish shopkeepers are very frightened of Hitler and many have left their businesses and fled into the country. Grandpa promised to send them some vegetables. They were grateful and asked if we had a sufficient stock of oil and candles. It seems that Grandpa wants to buy something he can lay his hands on. Grandpa knows from bitter experience that when there is a war, everything is in short supply.

Before sunset, Uncle Tadeusz and Aunt Aniela arrived bringing in a lot of valuable silver, glass, porcelain and other articles of sentimental value. Unfortunately, they also brought some bad news about our Baltic Corridor. The German Fourth Army has pushed through our defence lines. Uncle Tadeusz said that hundreds of Polish Cavalrymen lost their lives in a heroic battle. We were utterly sickened by this news. Grandpa suffered most. His empty eye-socket filled with tears. He blew his nose and went to the stable. Grandpa always goes to talk to Samson when things are bad.

13th September 1939

I very much hope that the thirteenth is more unlucky to the Gerries than it is to us. Warsaw is fighting back. We can hear explosions by day and see the red sky at night. Several shells have landed in nearby fields. Uncle Tadeusz decided that we'd have to build a shelter at the bottom of the garden. He thinks that our house might become a target for Nazi tanks. Having chosen a suitable place, Uncle Tadeusz got everybody he could grab hold of, including his wife, and formed us into a platoon. As the Commander-in-chief, he handed each of us a spade and told us to dig while he went elsewhere. Being next to Aunt Aniela, I could see that she is not a digger. Every time I dug a hole, she filled it in. After half-an-hour, which seemed like two hours, Uncle Tadeusz returned to inspect the hole. He was not pleased with our progress, and he said so. It is Uncle's nature to call a spade a spade and he did not mince his words on this occasion either. He wanted to know whether I and Aunt Aniela were, by any chance, digging for worms. I said that I was not, but Aunt Aniela said that she would much rather dig for worms than for Uncle Tadeusz. And to emphasize what she'd just said, she aimed her spade at the ground, but landed it on Uncle's foot. Uncle yelled and hobbled back towards the house in a huff. Aunt Aniela ran after him begging his forgiveness. We all agreed that it was a bad day for digging the shelter. We sank our spades in the ground and followed the Chief.

16th September 1939

Some good news today. The Germans have been repulsed on the Western Front. Our hopes rose and with them our moods improved. Uncle Tadeusz started to tease Mama and Aunt Stefa. He said that Mama puts on weight in front whereas Aunt Stefa does at the back, and it was quite out of character for identical twins to behave in such a contrary way. Aunt Stefa replied that he was a fine one to talk about other people's figures. Has he, meaning Uncle, by any chance, seen his own paunch? Uncle Tadeusz said he had, and it was not without purpose. Putting on weight around the middle kept him well balanced. Mama said that he was unbalanced because his head was too big. Everybody laughed, including Grandpa. Even Pempela wagged her tail. It was just like before the war. Mama made some cheese from the goat's milk. It looked delicious but nobody wanted to eat it. People just passed the cheese around and it came back to Mama untouched. She said it was the last time she was going to take the trouble to make cheese. Uncle Tadeusz, having made a sigh of relief, handed Mama pencil and paper and asked her to put it in writing. Everyone burst out laughing again, as if making the most of it before the next onset of doom.

18th September 1939

The shelter is ready. Uncle Tadeusz, having banished every female from the site, harnessed men to finish the job. Our shelter consists of a large hole in the ground which is lined with straw. The roof is made of logs, straw and earth. Papa said it was as depressing as a graveyard and a proper death-trap. And he, for one, won't be risking his neck by going in there. Uncle Tadeusz said that Papa might change his mind when a shell lands in his bed. Papa replied that he would much rather sleep with a shell than in Uncle's shelter. I said that I wanted to stay in the house too, but Mama ticked me off and said that I'll have to do what she says and not what I want to do. I felt cross with Mama and didn't like her just then. After ten-thirty in the evening, when the gun-fire intensified its rage, and when the moon climbed up the blue-black sky, we packed ourselves on the straw in the shelter like sardines. There was practically no room to lie down and not much air to breathe. The onion soup from supper was not a good idea, pointed out Uncle Tadeusz. At that moment he must have envied Papa, though he didn't say so. I asked Mama whether I could go back to my bed but she said "No", and in such a funny tone of voice that I did not dare to ask her again. Jurek complained that he couldn't breathe and Aunt Stefa told him to do without breathing. Every time somebody moved, a trickle of sand came down from the roof. Aunt Aniela said she felt like a mummy without having the advantage of being embalmed. Every quarter-of-an-hour somebody asked what was the time. By three in the morning, the atmosphere in the shelter got so heavy that if we stayed there a minute longer we would have suffocated. Aunt Aniela scrambled out first, saying that she'd much rather be blown to bits by a bullet than be poisoned by bad onions. We all followed, thankful for her courage. Mama could hardly stand up. She had a cramp in one leg and pins and needles in the other. We toddled off to the house, truly grateful for having a real roof over our heads and real beds to sleep in. Last night was the first time we used the garden shelter and it could well be the last. Very likely Uncle Tadeusz did not think much of his own architecture either, for he was just as pleased to get out of it.

19th September 1939

We are overwhelmed with sorrow. Polish resistance has collapsed. The Russians and the Germans have met near Brest Litovsk. Warsaw is on its last legs. Papa said that they are short of ammunition and food. The German propaganda is pouring in from every wavelength. Papa's been trying to get the BBC on his secret wireless set which is somewhere in the attic. Papa often goes up there with Aunt Aniela. He fiddles with the knobs and she takes everything down. Then Tadek and Wojtek distribute the news around the village.

This afternoon, Father Jakob called to see how we are getting on. Grandpa was full of indignation about God allowing such injustice to prevail on Polish soil. Father Jakob had to stop Grandpa before he said something terrible. When Grandpa gets going and when he's het up no-one is safe, not even God. Having soothed Grandpa's nerves, Father Jakob said that we, the children of God, are not here to question His wisdom but to pray for help and peace. Grandpa said that's exactly what he's been doing and a lot of good it did. Father Jakob replied that God has been awfully busy lately with everybody praying at the same time. Grandpa nodded and agreed that it must be sheer hell in Heaven, just now.

20th September 1939

Great-Uncle Emil came to see Grandpa to discuss the matter of guns and other weapons in the village. Grandpa suggested hiding them under the hay in the barn. But Uncle Tadeusz pointed out that it was the first place the Germans would search. He said the safest place for all weapons was underground. Later in the morning, Great-Uncle Emil and Anton brought in at least a dozen different guns and buried them somewhere in the garden. I only hope Uncle Tadeusz can remember what is buried where.

Anton heard from a friend that he had met a shepherd who had seen a German soldier near Zegrze. That's only three kilometres from us. So I went to a nearby field to see if I could spot any German soldiers. I saw nothing but heard enough to last me a long time. When I got about three hundred metres from the house, I heard bullets whistling around me. At first I didn't realise what was happening, until I saw puffs of dust in the road. Someone was shooting at me. Immediately I lay down on the ground, too petrified to move. My heart was thumping like mad. After a while the shooting stopped. I didn't know what to do. The Germans must be quite near, I reckoned. I started to crawl, almost slithering like a grass snake. My dress, my knees and my hands were covered in dust. After several minutes I heard a cow mooing. A bullet had gone through her hind leg. Blood was pouring down and the poor beast was in agony. By then I was really scared. I got up and ran as fast as I could. When I got to the house, filthy and out of breath, Mama was furious with me. Before I had the chance to explain what had happened she spanked me. I went to my room and cried and cried. But then I remembered the poor injured cow. So I went to tell Grandpa about it. He praised me and said it was an act of God that I saw the incident, otherwise the cow, belonging to Anton's sister-in-law, might have bled to death. At once Anton went to the cow with his first-aid kit. Afterwards, when Mama helped me to change and wash, I think she was sorry for spanking me so hastily for she hugged and kissed me and said that it was a silly thing to do. Papa was quite worried when he learnt how near the Germans are. He went up to the attic to hide the wireless set. For the time being, Papa put it underneath a pile of dirty washing. After tea, Uncle Tadeusz went to the attic and knocked several bricks out of the chimney stack and built a handy hideout for the wireless on the side facing the roof. It was a removable panel and it is almost invisible. Uncle Tadeusz said it was all right so long as no-one lit the fire in the south side of the house.

21st September 1939

Our capital is on fire. At night we can see the sky stained with smoke and flame. The guns have died down. German troops have surrounded Warsaw almost completely. Papa says it's only a matter of days. We feel thoroughly dejected, forsaken by justice. Why, oh why, are the Nazis winning the war?

25th September 1939

Nothing but bad news. People are prepared for the worst to happen. A convoy of German troops on the main road to Warsaw has been reported by one villager. Grandpa is in a state of continuous anxiety. Mama is worried about his health. She's been brewing a herbal potion for his nerves. The odour of valerian pervaded the whole house and Papa said that anyone who can survive its wicked smell can survive anything. Mama made the brew in a jug and insisted that

Grandpa should drink the lot. The effect was indisputable. Grandpa was flat out for the rest of the day. Mama got worried and wondered whether she'd cured him too much, and wanted to call the doctor. But Uncle Tadeusz said that, before getting better, it was quite natural for anyone to pass through a bad patch. Mama was not at all convinced, but she agreed that, at least, Grandpa's nerves were having a rest. After several hours, Grandpa was still passing through his bad patch. He remained in bed, sleeping it off, for two days. When the Germans came, Grandpa was beyond any fear, but the rest of us, quite literally, shivered in our boots. A full lorry-load of Gerries spilled out at our gate at the crack of dawn. They bashed on the front door, nearly knocking Uncle Tadeusz down, and rampaging through the house like a torrent of hoodlums. With their rifles at the ready, they poked and probed at anything and everything. Presumably, having found nothing they were looking for, they departed, leaving everybody alive, thank the Lord, but the house in a dreadful mess. After the visitation we all felt like a drop of Mama's valerian.

26th September 1939

Borowa-Góra is swarming with Gerries. There are at least two soldiers for every villager. Their uniforms are greenish-blue, and they are wearing black, knee-length boots. Some have helmets on their heads, others just forage caps, but all carry pistols hanging from their belts. The amazing part is that they feel quite at home in our village. They know exactly where to find food or water, how many men there are available for labour, and how many horses and carts there are at hand. They seem to know everything, though none, as far as I know, can speak Polish. Our German language is virtually non-existent. Uncle Tadeusz has a smattering of it and Aunt Aniela finds it not too difficult to guess what they say, German being somewhat similar to English. Though Papa feels it's useful to know *"nicht verstehen"*. So far, Herr Kommandant von Klein has only been wanting food, and he didn't ask for it, he just helped himself. Our cellar seems to have great fascination for Herr Kommandant. Fortunately, Mama and Aunt Stefa managed to smuggle out some of our precious preserves before they disappeared. Herr Kommandant set up his headquarters in the other house belonging to Grandpa which is usually let to holidaymakers, and which is situated near the main road to Warsaw. Thank goodness it's some distance from our house, and Papa still might be able to listen to an occasional news bulletin on his secret wireless.

28th September 1939

Warsaw surrendered yesterday. Mr Starzynski, the city mayor, has been shot by the Nazis. We feel appalled by this barbaric act. Grandpa took it very badly and asked for another dose of Mama's brew but she was somewhat reluctant to give it to him. Instead, Papa mixed him a vodka cocktail. Grandpa drank two glasses at once and a third one more leisurely. After that, he felt much better. So much so, that he went to see Herr Kommandant in his new headquarters and told him to clear out. Luckily for all of us, and even more so for Grandpa, Herr Kommandant had no idea what Grandpa was on about. Uncle Tadeusz, having learnt what Grandpa was up to, went to fetch him, explaining to the German commander that his father was suffering from mental aberration. Mama put Grandpa to bed and blamed Papa for everything. She said that vodka must have been invented by the devil himself, because it brings misery to so many. And pleasure to millions, pointed out Papa. Mama argued that all Papa does is to seek pleasure. To which Papa replied that he saw nothing wrong in enjoying himself. They argued for at least half-an-hour, by which time Grandpa got sober and Mama felt better for having made Papa miserable.

29th September 1939

Uncle Tadeusz has been trying to get to Warsaw but without any luck. The city is surrounded by German troops and no-one from the inside or the outside is allowed to cross the border. Apparently, the people of Warsaw are carrying on with their work as usual, in spite of the fact that many buildings have been completely destroyed, or burned down. Uncle is furious with the Gerries. He wants to know what has happened to his shops in Warsaw. The frontier between the city on the south side and the rest of the country is along the river Bug and the customs post, set up by the Germans, is at Zegrze. Uncle Tadeusz drove his Fiat as far as the bridge and there he was stopped. He had to show his credentials, the number of his car was taken, together with his name and address. At one stage, Uncle thought they would detain him. Luckily, he was released and lost no time driving back home as fast as he could. Gradually, we are learning to keep quiet and inconspicuous, but always hoping that tomorrow will bring a brighter outlook.

30th September 1939

Aunt Aniela has been summoned to cook dinners for Herr Kommandant at his headquarters in Grandpa's other house. Uncle Tadeusz tried to explain that his wife knew very little about cooking and suggested that Irka might suit him better. But the answer was no. Herr Kommandant knows exactly what he likes and Aunt Aniela was his choice. So she reported at his office just after six and was told to prepare pork chops, sauerkraut and potatoes for his supper. Aunt Aniela is as good at cooking as she is at digging, which amounts to very little. Not many people could produce a burnt glass of tea. Well, Aunt Aniela can, I know, because I've sampled it. Although we all felt sorry for her, Irka and I could not help giggling at the unlikely finesse of the cordon bleu meal prepared by Aunt Aniela. It serves Herr Kommandant right, and with a little bit of luck he might even choke.

3rd October 1939

A German soldier shot little Gabriel. We are sickened at this callous act of violence. The soldier came to tell us to report for potato picking next week. Gabriel doesn't like strangers and he could not resist nipping his leg. The soldier pulled out his revolver and shot Gabriel on the spot. The dog died instantly. Mama and Aunt Stefa are very upset. Uncle Tadeusz told Tadek to bury Gabriel somewhere in the garden. We wrapped him in a clean cloth and put him in a little coffin which Wojtek made from bits of wood. On the headstone, we inscribed the words: "Here lies little angel Gabriel who bit the big devil."

25th October 1939

I asked Father Jakob yesterday if it were a sin to be nasty to the Gerries. Father Jakob scratched his head and said that under normal circumstances it would be a sin. But, taking into consideration the fact that we are at war, or, to be more precise, the Germans are occupying our country, God probably would be prepared to give us some sort of dispensation. Then I asked him, even if I were to kill a German, would I not end up in Hell? Father Jakob said that in self-defence killing is permissible, but not premeditated killing. He wanted to know whether I followed him and I said that I did, which is a lie, because I didn't. In actual fact, the more I think about the sin of killing the less I understand the whole business. To me, a killed man, for whatever reason, is a dead man, and to him surely it doesn't matter why he had died? His only worry is that he's dead and he can't do anything about it. Then I asked Papa if he would consider pinching spuds from the Gerries a sin. Papa said it was most certainly not. He explained it to me like this: suppose a burglar stole my doll and I pinched it back. That wouldn't be stealing because the doll belonged to me in the first place. The same with the Germans. They have no right to be here. It is they who are the thieves. They are taking our crops from our fields and, on top of this, they are forcing us to work for them. Papa said it was a triple sin. I can always understand Papa and I hope God will remember to give the Gerries three bad marks.

5th November 1939

The Gerries have declared that the city of Warsaw is to be called a Protectorate. Papa wants to know who is going to protect whom and against whom? The primary schools and the commercial colleges will be opened, but no higher education such as gymnasiums, lyceums and universities. They will remain closed. Papa said that a well-educated Polish population is against the interests of the Nazis. All they want of us is to labour for them. This is something that we all should try to resist. We can't refuse to work but we can work at a snail's pace, Papa said.

This afternoon we've been digging out carrots and storing them in dry sand. This is a nasty job and I could hardly wait till the last lot was brought in by Papa and Uncle Tadeusz. We put the carrots in layers in wooden boxes. Then Uncle covered them with sand, then another layer, and so on, ending up with a layer of sand. By the time we'd finished the job, I'd had enough of carrots to last me for a long time. But no. Mama had the bright idea of giving us some more carrots for supper. It would do us good, she said, plonking on the table a huge dish of stewed carrots with microscopic pieces of rabbit. Fortunately there was an apple charlotte to follow and it did soften the blow, for me at any rate. As I grumbled so much about the first course, Mama gave me two slices of cake to keep me quiet.

14th November 1939

Papa held a secret meeting with four other men. I have never seen them before, but they were not strangers to Papa. They called him by his Christian name. I

think they must be papa's friends from Warsaw who
are interested in politics because after they'd finished
two rounds of vodka, they were listening to Papa's
wireless or maybe they put a new set in the place of
the old one. When they finished talking to Papa, they
didn't go out through the front gate, but they went
through a hole in the fence and disappeared into the
fields and then nearby woodland. I wanted to ask Papa
who they were, but one look at Papa's face told me it
would have been no good. I expect they must be some
sort of very secret agents.

26th November 1939

The Gerries have been deporting young men from
our village to work on the farms in Germany. They
need the labour. Mama is worried about the boys, but
Uncle Tadeusz reckons they're still too young. Papa
said that there is bad news from battles at sea. British
and Polish liners have been sunk by German mines.
Papa was so depressed that he went to bed early.
Grandpa said that if the Gerries win the war it won't
be worth living. If they win the war Poland will be lost
forever, that's what Grandpa said, and it made me very
sad.

14th December 1939

Papa says that the French and the British will attack
the Germans in the spring. We must wait and hope
and keep our fingers crossed. Meanwhile the people in
the villages are devising new ways of hiding food away
from the Gerries. Apparently, their army is like a
swarm of locusts, people say. Uncle Tadeusz made a

hide-out at the back of our barn. The barn has been partitioned and the entrance to the food-store has been camouflaged with bundles of straw. This is just in case our cellar gets raided by the Gerries. The longer we live with our enemies, the more we learn about their disregard for human lives and rights.

16th December 1939

When I got up this morning and looked out, I was dazed by the glistening glory. Ten centimetres of snow fell during the night and it seemed so fluffy and as light as duck's down. After a hasty breakfast I went outside to marvel at, and to touch, the snow. To me it is the eighth wonder of the world. Only snow has the cosmetic skill to turn an ugly eyesore into an object of sheer beauty. It also purifies the air. The sun has already climbed above the tops of the pines, eager to take a look at the new scene. The same lime trees which a while ago shivered in their trunks were standing so still, as if fearful of losing their newly acquired apparel. Every branch and every twig has been sprinkled with white. What a delight. I was reluctant to walk over this endless perfection. Almost afraid to spoil the vision of my sight's resurrection. There were tints of blue in the shade and the glow of pink where the sun stroked the snow. I stood amidst the wonderland hypnotised by its beauty, until Mama broke the spell. She said I'd catch my death without my winter coat.

19th December 1939

I am so stiff today that I can hardly move. Mama said it serves me right. Mama can be unfeeling at times.

She could show me some sympathy at least. The frost has eased and there is a thaw on the way. Wojtek's made a snowman which looks very much like Hitler. He made the moustache from an old broom, the eyes from a broken beer bottle and he put a swastika on his left arm. His right arm was raised in the Nazi salute. On his head, he had Grandma's old chamber-pot. We all laughed so much. Our Wojtek is really quite clever. Uncle Tadeusz, however, told Wojtek to demolish it. He said it was too much like the Führer and it was too dangerous. He reminded us what happened to little Gabriel. So we armed ourselves with sticks and bottles and had a go at Hitler with unbelievable pleasure. First went his arm, then his head hurtled off. His rounded belly was speared with a broomstick, and finally he collapsed, reduced to a mere heap of snow. Wojtek stuck a little white and red flag on top of the rubble signifying our victory. The three of us stood to attention and sang the Polish national anthem.

Dirk Van der Heide
(pseudonym)

12 YEARS OLD

HOLLAND

*D*irk Van der Heide, a twelve-year-old blue-eyed Dutch boy with taffy-colored hair, was living in Rotterdam with his mother, father, and little sister, Keetje, when the blitzkrieg of 1940 began. Encouraged by his mother, he began a diary of the terror he and his sister were living through.

Shortly after the German bombardment started, Dirk's father went off to fight the Nazis in another part of Holland. Then his mother was killed in an air raid. The children's uncle Pieter made the decision to try to transport Dirk and Keetje to safety in England. Despite tremendous odds, he was able to drive them from Rotterdam to the coast of Holland, where he secured passage for all of them on a boat to England.

The safety they gained by risking their lives at sea was all too brief. The bombing of London began just as they arrived there, and the children had to be evacuated once again. Dodging German submarines and mine fields, a "children's ship" took them to America.

Dirk used the time on the boat to rewrite and add to the diary he had kept of the nightmare he and his sister had experienced in Holland. It was translated and published in London and New York, in 1941, when Dirk was only thirteen years old. All the names in the book, including the author's, were changed, presumably because the

war was not over and the risk of Nazi persecution con-
tinued.

Friday, May 10, 1940

Something terrible happened last night. War
began!!! Uncle Pieter was *right*. The city has been
bombed all day. Am writing this in the Baron's air-raid
shelter. There are not many air-raid shelters here but
the Baron and Father and Mevrouw Klaes had this one
built for us and all our neighbors said it was a waste of
money. This has been a terrible day and everything is
upset and people are very sad and excited. This is what
happened. Before daylight I woke up and for several
minutes did not know what had happened. I could
hear explosions and people were shouting under our
windows. Mother came running in in her nightie and
dressing gown and told me to get my coat on and come
quickly. On the way downstairs she told me there was
bombing going on but no one knew yet what it meant
but she supposed it was war all right. The noise
seemed very near. Father had Keetje in his arms and
we hurried across the street to the Baron's and went
down into his air-raid shelter.

Father pointed toward the city and Mother nodded.
There were great flames shooting up into the sky and
beams of light from the searchlights and the sirens
were going very loud. They are on the tops of buildings
and have things on them to make them very loud. We
could see bullets going up from our guns. The Baron's
air-raid shelter was full of people, all our neighbors
and some people I didn't know. They were all talking
loudly and no one was dressed, just coats over their

nightclothes. Keetje began to cry and Father whispered something to her and kissed her and she stopped. Finally she went to sleep in his arms. We waited about two hours. At first most people thought the noise was only practice. All the time people kept running outside and coming back with news. It was war all right and the radio was giving the alarm and calling all the time for all men in the reserves to report for duty at the nearest place. The radio said this over and over. It was very exciting. The bombing kept on all the time, boom—boom-boom, and everyone said they were falling on Waalhaven, the air-port, which is only about five miles away. The Baron went upstairs and began telephoning. The voices on the radio sounded strange and terribly excited. Father put Keetje into Mother's arms and went away. A few minutes later he came back dressed and carrying a gas mask and a knapsack. He kissed Mother and Keetje and me very hard and then hurried out. He shouted back something about taking care of his animals and Mother nodded and told him to be careful, *please*.

All afternoon we waited around not doing much but listening to the grown-ups talk and listening to the radio. People are all very kind to each other and friendly, even the ones who don't speak to each other usually. By five o'clock half of the fifty people at the Baron's house had gone home or run away in their cars to the country or somewhere. Anyway they were not around.

We got up a game with several other children playing soldiers and bombers. We took turns jumping off the high back steps holding umbrellas and pretending we were parachutists but we had to quit this because

the grown-ups said it made them nervous. Just as it
was getting dark the bombing started again. Mother
came home on a bicycle which was not hers. She had
taken the car in the morning but she said the roads
were being barricaded and it was quicker to come by
bicycle. We asked her many questions but she didn't
talk much. She looked tired and white faced when she
came into the air-shelter. The Baron and neighbors
have brought in many cots and mattresses and a small
electric stove on which coffee urns stand. It is damp
and uncomfortable in the small shelter with so many
people. It was all right this morning but it is not pleasant as time goes by. There are four old sick people near
the stove but I don't know any of them. The old sick
people keep their eyes closed most of the time. Once
in a while someone speaks to them and pulls the blankets up when they slip down. They are very silent and
tired and dead looking.

LATER

The air-raid that came this time lasted 30 minutes.
It was no better than the others but no worse. The
Baron brought down a Victrola and turned it on full
blast to try to shut out the noise outside. Some of the
music was German music, Mother said. How could it
be from the same race who were attacking us she
asked. The radio was off during the raid but it started
up soon afterwards. The Premier of Holland, Dirk Jan
de Geer, spoke and said for us to be confident because
the Allies would help us and that hundreds of troops
had been landed at Hoogezwaluwe, the big bridge
which is between north and south Holland. When he
finished, the radio said the landing field at Schiphol

airdrome had been destroyed. Everyone was sad about this for it is our largest field. Had supper at the Baron's and settled down for the evening. All the lights have gone out upstairs and we are burning candles and lanterns down in the air-shelter.

Mother called the hospital after the last raid and Uncle Pieter but Uncle Pieter's hotel didn't answer. It is very hard to get anyone on the telephone. Everyone is calling everyone else after the raids are over to see if they are safe. The telephones are off during the raids. I hope Uncle Pieter is safe and Father too. Mother thinks Father has gone east to Maastricht and that's where the fighting is thickest the radio says though the bombing is bad everywhere.

Saturday, May 11, 1940

The worst air-raid of all has just come. About half the houses on our street are gone. One bomb landed on the lawn by our air-shelter and one side of the shelter is caved in but the Baron and others are repairing it now. Mevrouw Hartog broke down and cried during the air-raid and got everyone very nervous when she yelled. I think she almost went crazy.

Heintje Klaes was killed! He went outside to see the light from the big flares and incendiary bombs and didn't come back. He slipped out. Heintje was not afraid of anything but the bombs got him. The whole house rocked when the bombs came close. We put our fingers in our ears but it didn't help much. The fire wagons are working outside now and half the people in the air-shelter including Uncle Pieter have gone out. I went out for a while and they were taking dead peo-

ple out of the bombed houses. Uncle Pieter sent me
back to stay with Keetje. There is a funny smell in the
air like burnt meat and a funny yellow light all over
the country from the incendiary bombs. Three men
were killed trying to get a bomb away that hadn't gone
off yet. One of the men was our postmaster and I loved
him very much. He gave me my first bicycle ride. It is
awful to watch the people standing by their bombed
houses. They don't do much. They just walk around
and look at them and look sad and tired. I guess there
isn't anything else they can do, but it seems awful.

Our house wasn't hit but the street in front of it
between our house and the Baron's is just a great big
hole and all the cobblestones are thrown up on our
lawn and the Baron's until it doesn't look as if there
ever was a street there. Mother is going to be surprised
when she sees it. The street was just made over last
year and was very smooth and nice.

At the end of our street the water is coming in
where the canal locks were hit and I guess it will just
keep running over the land until it is fixed. No one
does anything about it because there are too many people to be helped and fires to fight. Twelve people on
our street were killed and I knew every one of them
but I knew Heintje best. Mevrouw Klaes has been crying ever since the bombing. Some people prayed all the
time and some sang the national anthem and some just
sat and stared. A woman who is very sick with a bad
heart looked as if she might die. She was very pale
when she came and still is.

I said a prayer to myself for Father and I hope God
heard it in spite of all the noise. I told Uncle Pieter I
had prayed but he didn't say anthing, just laid his hand

on my shoulder. Uncle Pieter has gone off to the hospital to try to find Mother. It is getting late and he is worried I think. I know he will find her. Keetje has gone to sleep again but she talks in her sleep and wakes up all the time, asking if the war is over and things like that. Poor Keetje, she is so little and doesn't know what is happening. I think I do and it is worse than anything I ever heard about and worse than the worst fight in the cinema. The ambulances coming and going and so many dead people make it hard for me not to cry. I did cry some while the bombing was going on but so many other little children were that no one noticed me I think. I just got into bed with Keetje and hid my face. I was really frightened this time.

LATER

Uncle Pieter came back. He didn't find Mother because she is dead. I can't believe it but Uncle Pieter wouldn't lie. We aren't going to tell Keetje yet. The ambulances are still screaming. I can't sleep or write any more now or anything.

Sunday, May 12, 1940

I am writing this in the morning as Keetje and I wait for Uncle Pieter. He is taking us to Dordrecht and then to Zeeland if we can get there. I can't believe Mother is dead and that we will never see her again. Mother was killed when the hospital was bombed. I cried almost all night and I am ashamed of what I did in front of everybody. I tried to run away from Uncle Pieter after he told me about Mother getting killed. I tried to get out in the street to fight the Germans. I don't know what all I did. I was crazy. I was all right until the bombs started to fall around midnight and then I couldn't stand it. I know I yelled and kicked and bit Uncle Pieter in the hand but I don't know why. I think I was crazy. I went to sleep later but I don't know what time it was.

Today I am tired but everyone is so kind.

Monday, May 13, 1940

The fires on the street are not all out yet. The air is still full of smoke and now the house is smoky inside. No one is talking very much today. Two of the old people died last night during the bombing. They were not hit by bombs. They just died. I heard the Baron say it's just as well. The Baron is sad today and his face, which is usually red and jolly, looks white and he has great dark circles under his eyes. The radio this morning says the Germans have come far into Holland and they are getting most of the bridges that aren't blown up. I don't know how Uncle Pieter expects us to get to Zeeland. No one understands why Holland is losing the war so easily. The first day people said we could hold out until the French and English would come. The Germans are using many new tricks, I think. A man came in this morning and said the Germans had taken one of our forts in the east by using a new kind of gas that makes the Dutch soldiers numb. Someone else said, Mijnheer van Helst, I think, that the Germans have a bomb so big that it tears up a whole city block at one time. He said the Germans have a fire thrower now that shoots out a long line of fire for a great distance. Almost everyone seems to think that the new kinds of guns and things the Germans have are the cause of all the trouble, but Uncle Pieter doesn't think so. He says they just have more of everything, that's all. Our defenses are fine he says except we didn't have enough anti-aircraft guns or planes. We are like every other country the Germans have beaten he says. We weren't expecting the war from the air or parachutists or tricks like that. Brenda has just come in with our traveling bags. We have to wait for Uncle Pieter. Brenda brought Dopfer, Keetje's big doll. Dopfer is very big and Keetje shouldn't try to take him but she wants to. She has been asking Brenda when Mother is coming, and is Mother going with us.

About three o'clock some German planes came over. They were seaplanes going toward Dordrecht. They dropped no bombs but five of them dived down toward the road until we thought they were falling and then they shot at us with machine guns. We all got under the car and many people crawled in beside us. Other people threw themselves on the ground and dived into the roadside ditches for protection. The soldiers tried to shoot the pilots with their rifles. The planes kept going back and forth above us very low and loud and then suddenly they went away south. There was great confusion after they left. Several people were hit. One woman in front of us, a young woman, sat by the roadside holding her head and groaning. There was blood coming out of her head and a hole in the side. It made me sick. About fifty people were wounded and many were killed. Uncle Pieter helped the wounded all he could and then we hurried away. All the way down the road we saw wounded people and people just lying still in the road.

Once Uncle Pieter had to get out and move three bodies to the side to get by. It was awful. Many children were crying. People were trying to be brave and pretend nothing had happened but they were all very sad and angry. The Germans are cowards to shoot people who have no guns. When they drop bombs they don't know where they go but they just came down on the road and shot at us today. I hope those Germans in those planes fall out of the sky and never get home and are killed. There are no towns along the Dordrecht-Rotterdam highway for the poor wounded people to get to. Nothing more happened until we got near Dordrecht and then we heard firing again. We were stopped and had our papers looked at and told not to go into the city but to go around it as there was fighting in the center of the city because of the Dordrecht bridges and the parachutists who were there.

Tuesday, May 14, 1940

Uncle Pieter must have been very clever to get us on the boat with so many trying to get on. We have been on the boat an hour but it hasn't left yet. It is late at night. There are no lights on the outside of the boat but inside there is some light but the portholes are covered. The boat has started and I wish I could go out on deck. But this is not permitted.

LATER

The boat slipped along in the darkness and we could hardly see a thing through the cabin windows. There is not a single light in Vlissingen because of the bombers. I wonder if the little boy and girl we left at the café in Dordrecht are all right now. I hope so. I feel very sorry for them. There are many people on the boat. No one talks, for it is against the rules. There are no beds for us and we have to sit up but Uncle Pieter has taken Keetje up in his arms and she is asleep now.

LATER

I've been asleep for several hours. I woke up a little while ago. I had a terrible nightmare about bombing and I thought a bomber was chasing me and Keetje around and around the canals and we were on ice-skates and kept slipping and falling and couldn't get away. The nightmare was terrible. I was cold when I woke up and Uncle Pieter wrapped his big coat around me. We are sailing on.

LATER

The boat has been tossing around a great deal. I asked Uncle Pieter how long it will take to get to England. He says a good while because we have to go back and forth zigzag to get through the mine fields in the water. I am scared we might hit one and sink. I can't swim very well and Keetje can't swim more than ten strokes without puffing. Uncle Pieter says not to think about it. I try not to but I keep thinking about it. I was very frightened when I heard a loud explosion ahead of us some time later. Our boat slowed down after that. I thought the bombers had come again but there was nothing in the sky. The boat's searchlights went on for a few seconds but I couldn't see what had happened. We found out a few minutes later. The boat ahead of us had struck a mine and been blown up. Our boat tried to pick up a few people from the water and did pick up some but not many. The Captain of the boat tried to find the others but he couldn't find many because he didn't want to have the lights on. I hate to think of all the people out there swimming in the cold sea while we are going on to England. I hope they don't all drown. This war is terrible. It kills just about everybody. I'm glad we're going to England where it will be quiet. I hope the Germans don't come there the way they did in Holland. I don't feel very well tonight. I have a bad headache and my stomach feels funny. Maybe I am going to be seasick but I think it's just from the bombing and everything. I forgot to say how nice Keetje was before we left Dordrecht. She gave her big doll, Dopfer, to the little girl. Keetje was nice to do this. She is often very selfish but she was good to do this. It seems funny to be out here on our way to England. I have always wanted to go to England but I never thought I would go so soon. I pray God will keep our Father safe. We could not bear to lose Father after what happened to Mother. Uncle Pieter is very good to take care of us while Father is away fighting the Germans.

Wednesday, May 15, 1940

We have been in England all morning. It was daylight almost when our boat got in. We landed at a place called Harwich. Everyone cheered and sang when we came into the harbor safely. We took the train to London, which took about three hours, and went to a place in the station where refugees have to go. There were many English people there to give us breakfast and to help us. They were all very cheerful and smiling.

Some of the refugees looked ill and very unhappy and lost. There were children there without any parents or relatives or friends. Some of the children were French and Belgian. There were several English doctors there and some of them spoke Dutch. They were helping to fix wounded people. Uncle Pieter has taken us to a hotel near the station. I am writing this in the hotel. Uncle Pieter says most of the Dutch and Belgian and French refugees are going to the country away from London so that if the bombs come again they will be safe. They will go to Ireland and Yorkshire and the Isle of Man and places like that where I have never been.

LATER

Uncle Pieter has just come back with terrible news. Holland has surrendered to the Germans. It is all in the newspapers. Uncle Pieter is almost crying. Ever since he came in he has been drinking and smoking and walking up and down. He says the fall of Holland threatens England and we must go to America if we can get a boat. Queen Wilhelmina, the paper says, is going to speak over the radio but we have no radio and cannot hear her. Uncle Pieter says maybe he won't be able to get back to Holland or find out any news of anything. I wonder where Father is. I hope he is all right and safe and can go back to doctoring his animals. I just asked Uncle Pieter if we couldn't go back now that the war is over and he said never, never could we go back there while the Germans were there. He says it is worse than death for Hollanders to live as slaves. I hope the Germans don't make a slave out of

Father. I don't think they could. Father gets very angry and he would not stand for it.

Keetje is feeling very tired and ill. Uncle Pieter is having some food sent up to her, some warm milk and toast and eggs. I am having roast beef and pudding here with Keetje and Uncle Pieter is going to eat later. We haven't seen much of London yet and we have to stay inside tomorrow and rest. This is a very large room with high ceilings. Keetje and I stay in here and Uncle Pieter stays beyond the double doors. We have a private bath and it is very nice and quiet. The windows are all covered with thick cloth because it is after dark and no light must be shown because of the Germans. Keetje says she hopes there won't be any noise tonight and that the Germans had better not come to London.

Monday, July 1, 1940

We have been in England many weeks. Now we are in Liverpool waiting for a boat to America. Uncle Pieter has heard from Uncle Klaas in America and he wants Keetje and me to come. Uncle Klaas had to cable the American Consul and his bankers in America had to do the same thing. Uncle Pieter had to get visas and things and all kinds of papers and pay a great deal of money, I think. A great fuss. We are having much fun in England but we miss Holland. Keetje was ill for a week in the hotel in London. A doctor came to see her and said she was nervous. He gave her some medicine. He was very kind. He wouldn't let Uncle Pieter pay him anything. He said it was his pleasure and his gift to gallant Holland. Uncle Pieter argued with him but the kind doctor said no. Uncle Pieter says the English are just that way and good enough people when you know them.

Dear Uncle Pieter. He is so sad about Holland and so good to us. We have done so many things. In London he took us everywhere. The policemen—*bobbies* they are called!—are very funny and big and polite. We asked them many questions on walks when we got lost. We used to take taxis everywhere but now we use the little trams. All over London there are many things for war. Sand-bags everywhere. They were banked around the British Museum the day we went. The Museum has big pillars outside and many heavy doors before you get inside. Uncle Pieter was surprised to see so many people inside reading while there is a war on. There are many trenches everywhere and sand-bags at St. Paul's, a big church. In the gardens of Kensington there were many flowers but trenches too.

There are big black and white posters everywhere with ARP printed on them. This means Air Rapid Precautions. People all carry gas-masks and we have them now. They were fitted on us by a nice woman in London. The gas masks have long snouts and look as funny as the Dutch ones. They have straps to hold them on. We must never carry them by the straps because they stretch and might let the gas in. That's what the woman said who gave them to us. Uncle Pieter put his on yesterday for the first time and looked at himself. He said he looked no better at all with it than without it. I laughed and he laughed too. I was glad to see him laugh for he has been so sad since he found out that one-fourth of our army was killed. When he reads the newspapers about the war he gets sadder and sadder. We haven't heard from Father.

When Belgium fell Uncle Pieter was almost sick. I saw a funny dog today. It was an English sheepdog, Uncle Pieter said. Keetje thought it was a bear that had escaped from the zoo. Keetje asked if the animals had gas masks too and Uncle Pieter said no. It is a shame they don't have. We had tea at the zoo with bread and butter and strawberry jam. I tasted Keetje's milk and it was good but not so good as the milk from the Baron's cows.

There are no street lights in England after dark. We are getting very tired of the dark but not as tired as we were. We have only been out once late at night. We were in a taxi with Uncle Pieter coming home from the Mickey Mouse cinema. There are no crossing lights except little shaded crosses no bigger than a button. It is very exciting going along in the dark. In the daylight we have gone into the country. The roads are all fixed to stop the Germans. There are many barricades and trenches and tank traps. We have seen many lorries in the streets with big searchlights and guns and soldiers.

Uncle Pieter has just come in with news. He says I must stop writing now. He has just had news from the ticket office that we have a passage and will leave sometime soon. He says he cannot go to see us off as it is against the rules because of the war. The ticket man is sending someone for us. I asked him the name of the boat and he said he didn't know that either because the ticket office couldn't let any secrets out because of the Germans. I must stop and help Keetje and Uncle Pieter pack. I hate to leave England. I have had a good time here and I hope the Germans never do to England what they did to Holland. Good-by, England. We have to leave you just as we were beginning to love you. I suppose we will have to get used to having new homes since we can't go back to our own dear home in Holland.

Wednesday, July 3, 1940

We are on the boat now. We sailed yesterday sometime after dark. We had to wait many hours on the dock with the ticket man who told us animal stories. It was hard to leave Uncle Pieter. He kissed us many times and hugged us hard. He is going to let us know about Father if he gets back to Holland. Uncle Klaas will meet us in New York. We are on a big boat and there are many other children going to America. There are so many people going away because of the war that some of them have to sleep in bunks in the smoking rooms and halls. Everything is very strict on this English boat. Before we sailed a sailor told us what we could do and what we couldn't. We are not allowed on deck after the trumpet sounds in the evening. All the portholes are fastened tight and can't be opened. They are covered with thick cloths to blot out the light. The ship doesn't even have lights on it to see by at night because of the submarines. The English sailor said no one could smoke on deck at night. A lighted cigarette can be seen two miles at sea, he says. If anyone disobeys he will be severely punished and put in a room and locked up for the rest of the trip.

There are double doors at the dining salon and we go in on the side so the lights don't show. There are many ships sailing beside us. We counted twenty. Six carry passengers and the rest are going along to keep the submarines away. There are torpedo boats, war-

ships, and one airplane carrier. They keep very near us
all the time and we wave back and forth. The boats are
all painted gray so they will be hard to see in the water.
Everyone is afraid of the German submarines. The English Captain says for me not to worry because anyone
who was born around as much water as we have in
Holland just couldn't be drowned. He is a nice man
and is always making jokes. There are two other Dutch
children on the boat. They came from The Hague.
Their father is working for the government. We speak
Dutch together just to rest our tongues. We practice *J*'s
and *th*'s on each other. Keetje has been seasick ever
since we left but the Captain says she will be better
when we get away from Ireland. He says he will be too
because most of the submarines stay around here.

I have never been on such a big boat. I have been on
many boats on canals but this one is like the Adelphi
Hotel in Liverpool only it wobbles. A man was caught
smoking a cigarette today and put into a room and
locked up just as the sailor said he would be. Many
boys in Holland smoke at my age but I do not. There
goes the bell for dinner and I am very hungry, and
Keetje is pulling at my sleeve. She feels like eating tonight.

Saturday, September 28, 1940

I have not written in my diary for so long. Not since
I got to America. Uncle Klaas and Aunt Helen met us.
Aunt Helen is an American with long red fingernails
and a very pretty face. Our boat came in to New York
at night on the tenth day after we left England. We
came slowly because our boat had to take a longer way

because of the war. We stayed all night in the harbor. There were so many lights and they were all on. All during the time we were in England there had never been any lights at night in the streets. It looked fine to see so many all going at once with so many colors. Uncle Klaas took us off the boat the next morning without waiting. Some of the children who were ill had to be taken off the boat somewhere else and some had gone to a place called Ellis Island.

When we got through the customs we drove to Uncle Klaas's apartment on Morningside Heights. The streets were very exciting. I remember particularly when we crossed one and Uncle Klaas said this is Broadway. I came over here just to show you, he said. Aunt Helen said it is prettier at night. Uncle Klaas has a beautiful apartment that is very near the river. Maybe he took it because he is Dutch and always wants to be near some water.

We have been in America several weeks now. Keetje and I go to a private school. We like it very much although it was strange at first. There were many new words and studies, but not so many languages to learn as in Holland. I am learning to play football and other sports. Keetje likes the movies and the drugstore sodas best. Keetje seems very happy. Sometimes I think she has forgotten about Mother entirely. But I haven't. Everyone is very kind to us and I have been made a monitor at school. School hours are shorter in America. My English has improved and I have learned many new words that I never heard in England and some not in my dictionary.

Several letters have come from England from Uncle Pieter. He has not been able to get back to Holland. He is working for the English now and is a volunteer fire warden. Uncle Pieter says he misses us. He has had one letter from Father and we have had one. Father is safe and back in Rotterdam. The letter we got from him had a Swiss stamp. It must not have been seen by the Germans, Uncle Klaas says. Father tells about what Holland is like now. There is not much food and many things like coffee and cocoa cannot be bought. The Germans have done many things. They have changed the names of the Royal Museum and anything with the word "royal" in it to National. No taxis are running. None of the Dutch can listen on the radio to anything but Spanish, Italian and German programs without being fined 10,000 guilders and two years in prison. People have to stay home after 10 o'clock at night. The food is getting worse and worse. Father said not to worry, he would pull through. He wants to come to America. I wish he could and so does Keetje. We write to him often but we don't know whether he gets our letters. I will be so glad when the war is over.

Keetje and I are happy here and everything would be perfect if Father and Grandfather and Grandmother were here and of course Uncle Pieter. I haven't had very good marks at school. The doctor says I am nervous and can't concentrate very well yet because of the bombing but that I will be all right later. The American doctor was just like the English one Uncle Pieter had for Keetje. He wouldn't charge any money for taking care of me. He said, *this is on me,* which is slang but very kind. I think he is a good doctor for I know I *am* nervous sometimes.

Sometimes when airplanes go over I want to run and hide. One night when it was raining I woke up and heard the rain on the glass and was frightened. I thought I was back in Holland and that what was striking the windows were pieces of bombs. That is why Uncle Klaas doesn't like it when people ask me about the war. When he saw the theme I was trying to write in English for my English class about the war in Holland he was angry. I heard him tell Aunt Helen that he thought it was dreadful and that he wanted Keetje and me to forget about the war. But I know I'll never forget about it anyway, or forget the Germans and how Mother died. I won't forget America either. It is a good country that has made us feel welcome. Keetje is looking over my shoulder as I write this and says why don't you say it's "swell," that's an American word.

I know one reason why I'll always love America. It's because of something that happened on the boat trip here. When we were one day away from New York all the battleships and boats that had brought us over so safely turned around and went back toward England. We were all alone and very frightened. I was frightened because I don't swim very well and Keetje can only do ten strokes and they don't get her very far. When the boats all turned back we could see how frightened everyone was. That's what made us frightened. We weren't frightened before. But then someone started yelling and pointing at the sky. There was a big zeppelin over us. It said United States Naval Patrol Number 14 in big letters. We all yelled and cheered. I won't ever forget that number 14, and the nice safe way it made us feel. The zeppelin followed us and watched over us all the rest of the way to America. And people have been watching over us ever since and there haven't been any bombings. Not one. And that is why Keetje and I are happy now.

Janina Heshele

12 YEARS OLD

POLAND

*J*anina Heshele was almost twelve years old when she began writing in her diary on the day the Germans took over Lvov, the Polish city in which she lived. Soon after, her father was taken by the Nazis and never seen again. She and her mother changed their names and tried to hide from the Gestapo, but they were eventually discovered and imprisoned in the Janowska death camp. Knowing the horrors that awaited her, Janina begged her mother to let her take a cyanide capsule and die. But her mother steadfastly refused to allow her to commit suicide.

Janina endured terrible conditions in Janowska, but then a miracle occurred in 1943. A group of prisoners who were extremely impressed by her writing, particularly her poetry, determined that her talent was so great that they could not allow it to be consumed in the Nazi ovens. By pooling their efforts, they were able to help her escape to the Aryan side of Cracow, where she survived the war and lived to see her diary published.

What follows are excerpts translated by Azriel Eisenberg (from a Hebrew translation of a part of Janina's diary), which appeared in his book The Lost Generation: Children in the Holocaust. Janina's diary was originally published in Polish by one of her rescuers, Maria Hochberg Marianska, but it is so rare today that no library in the world reports having it.

➤➤◄◄

1941–1943 [Dates unknown]

On the second day of the invasion, Father and I went out to view Lvov after the enemy's bombing. The city was unrecognizable; the stores had been destroyed and plundered by the populace. The houses were decorated with blue-and-yellow flags. Automobiles and cycles ornamented with flowers rolled through the streets, their drivers and fellow travelers jubilant.

Father, sensing he was in grave danger, kissed me and said, "Yanya, you are a grown person and from now on you have to be independent, fully on your own. Do not pay attention to what others say or do. Be strong and of good courage." He kissed me again and was about to part from me when I began to grasp what would happen and started to cry. But Father declared sternly, "If you love me, leave me. Be brave. Never cry. Crying is degrading. Return home immediately and leave me here." I gave Father a last kiss. At the street corner I looked back and I saw him returning a flying kiss to me.

[Janina's father is caught in the dragnet of the doomed and is never seen again. Janina goes underground and assumes a Polish name.]

One day a strange woman came to see me. I thought she had a message from Yadjah [a Christian friend], but she did not. She said to me, "I serve in the Gestapo. Your name is Janina Heshele but you pass as Lydia Wirischinska. If you don't bring me 5000 gulden by four o'clock, you will be sent to death at Camp Janowska." I ran to inform my uncle, and he transmitted the message to Mother. At four the woman showed up, and so did Mother. Mother knew intuitively that she was an extortionist. After a little haggling, the "lady" left with 100 gulden. [Janina and her mother go into hiding but are caught.]

We were brought to prison and pushed into a small, crowded cell where we found sixty people squatting on the floor, one on top of another. When we were thrust in, someone growled, "Oh, another herring!" Another replied, "Two in one." Mother did not let me lie on the floor, and we stood upright a full day and night.

In the morning, coffee and bread were brought in. Everyone had to pay for the food and drink. But Mother and I could not swallow our food. Even though it was the month of February, the cell was hot and stank. In the corner was a broken bucket where women and men attended to their physical needs. I had no strength to stand on my feet any longer, but Mother would not let me lie down for fear of my becoming infected with lice. I argued with her, asserting that I wished to catch typhus, for I couldn't bear to live any longer. I lay down on the floor. Mother did too, but since there was no room for both of us, she had me lie on top of her.

The day for deportation arrived. We knew our end was near. The anticipation was unbearable. We wished it were over. We knew we were doomed. I lost all control of myself and wept without stopping. I did not fear my own death so much, or even the shooting of the children, but the terror of seeing children buried alive was too great. Some prayed and chanted in Hebrew. A number of us prayed to be shot immediately. Mother calmed me down and promised that she would blindfold me when the shooting began. My panic subsided and I joined in chanting with the other victims.

About three in the morning a policeman came and asked Mother to come out with him. He inquired if there was a child with her. We both went out into the corridor and were taken to another cubicle. Here we were prohibited from loud talk and not allowed even to sneeze. On Saturday, at seven in the morning an automobile arrived to remove those condemned to die. . . . Periodically, five of us were taken to the basement, where we heard shots. We were saved. When they led us outside and I breathed the fresh air, I fell to the ground like one intoxicated.

[Janina falls ill with typhus and is taken to the hospital where her mother works.]

Mother, who was deathly pale, lay in bed. I lay down near her and asked her "Why are you so crushed? I am still alive." She replied, "I do not care what happens to me. I have a poison tablet which will bring instant death. But what will happen to you?" She broke out in loud sobs and implored me, "Anula, save me from further anguish. Go away. I don't want you near me. I don't want to see what will happen to you."

But I refused, saying, "What have I to live for? Without documents I cannot exist on my own. Mother, do you want to prolong my agonies? Isn't it better to make an end to my life once and for all? Let us die together, with me in your arms. Why live on?" Mother implored me, "You must go on! You must live to vindicate Father's death and mine."

My struggle with Mother robbed me of my strength. I could not glance at Mother's face because overnight it had become a network of wrinkles. She looked like my grandmother. I could hear her loud heartbeats. I gave in on condition that she give me a pill of potassium cyanide, but she refused. She gave me 2700 gulden, accompanied me to the exit, kissed me, and whispered to me, "Bear up for Mother's sake."

I begin to understand why my fellow victims go to their deaths without resistance. I have lost the desire to exist and feel a deep disgust for living. . . .

A day before the Jewish New Year all the sick patients were sent to the death chamber. Urland, the Jewish police officer, greeted us loudly, "I bless all of you with a New Year of Freedom." All of us, including Urland, wept. . . .

At the table sat Mrs. Jacobowitz, who had lit two candles which stood before her. Around her women crowded, exchanging New Year's blessings with one another and crying loudly. With composure, Mrs. Jacobowitz returned the blessings to each one. I could not bear to witness the scene and walked out.

A day before the great fast [Day of Atonement], we arranged a party with singing and constrained dancing. Urland prepared for each of us a repast of soup, two slices of bread, and an apple.

When we returned to our dormitories, night had fallen. The women lit candles and ushered in Yom Kippur with the appropriate blessings, accompanied by copious tears. I looked closely at the candles, at the halos ringing the burning wicks, and suddenly I felt a deep intuition that, despite it all, God is still with us. He sees how we give Him thanks for living, in spite of the horrors around us. I believed that ultimately He would not let the few remnants of Israel be wiped out.

I lay down on my bunk and asked myself, "Shall I

fast?" I was uncertain. Fasting was a Jewish religious ritual, and I *am* a Jewess. I did not want to ponder long and deep, because I felt that if I did so, I would reaffirm my disbelief in God. I was persuaded that faith in God bears with it the hope to live. I decided to fast. . . .

From the showers the prisoners go to eat. On the tables are pots of soup, but no one tastes a spoonful. Ten men [a religious quorum for prayer] enter. Urland locks the door, and the Jews begin the prayer service. A few women draw forth paper leaves—remnants of prayerbooks—and recite the Yizkor [Memorial Service for the Dead]. Others repeat after them, and all weep in unison. But as for me—my doubts reawake and reassail me. Why should I fast? Does God really exist? My former doubts return and shatter my erstwhile faith.

Winter is upon us, savage and murderous. I am cold as ice and can't sleep. My benefactors give me strength to persevere and console me that I will yet find safety on the Aryan side of Cracow. I cannot persuade myself to believe them. All mankind is egotistic. They think first of themselves and of their own welfare. I have no strength to hold up, to hope, to live. But in my ears there still echo the last words of my mother. "Carry on, do not despair, for your mother's sake!" Only these words keep the spark of life aglow within me.

Helga Kinsky-Pollack

13 YEARS OLD

AUSTRIA

Born in Vienna in 1930, Helga Kinsky-Pollack was deported to the Terezín transport camp (in what is now the Czech Republic) when she was thirteen. She was separated from her parents and subjected to fierce discipline, disease, hunger, and overcrowding. From Terezín, Helga was sent to Auschwitz and then forced into slave labor in the Flossenbürg concentration camp. Finally, she was returned to Terezín just before liberation. Helga survived all this and was able to hold on to the diary she had written during her first imprisonment in Terezín. The following are a few of her entries from 1943, which were translated into English and published in the book Terezín *in 1965.*

Tuesday, March 16, 1943

. . . I went to see my uncle in the Sudeten barracks and there I saw them throw out potato peelings and ten people threw themselves on the little pile and fought for them . . .

Friday, April 2, 1943

This day is filled with joy. The Germans themselves admit their losses at the front. This afternoon I moved to another bunk, in the bottom tier next to Ella Steiner. I'm happy. I had an unpleasant neighbour, Marta Kenderová, who always scolded me if I sat on her bunk . . .

Tuesday, April 6, 1943

Tomorrow SS-man Guenther is coming and no children can go out on the street tomorrow. Daddy doesn't know this and I'll die of hunger by evening . . .

Wednesday, April 7, 1943

I missed Daddy yesterday, but I didn't give in to my sadness, because the other children couldn't see their parents either and won't see them all day.

Saturday, April 10, 1943

We aren't allowed to go out of the barracks. We can't go into the street without a pass and children don't get a pass. They say this can last a week or even several months. I thought I wouldn't see Daddy for a long time, but he has been to see me twice. I seem like a bird in a cage. This is all because two prisoners escaped from the ghetto . . .

Thursday, May 6, 1943

It's terrible here in Terezín. A regular Tower of Babel. There are Germans, Austrians, Czech, Dutch, some French, I even know a Finnish girl, etc. There are Aryans, Jews and mixed. Next to my bunk there was a girl Antonie Michalová to whom fate was very cruel. She arrived three weeks ago from Brno; her father is an Aryan and her mother Jewish. She is completely alone, badly provided for, and does not feel right in a Jewish environment. She cries almost all day long. Her father was allowed to accompany her to Prague, where there was a terrible leave-taking, according to the account of a girl who came with her.

Saturday, July 31, 1943

This is the second day I've been sleeping in the corridor because of bedbugs. There are seven of us girls sleeping outside and we've all been bitten.

We have permission to sleep in the garden, because it's impossible in the corridor. Spraying with Flit didn't help at all. I caught six fleas and three bedbugs today. Isn't that a fine hunt? I don't even need a gun and right away I have supper. A rat slept in my shoe. Walter, our Hausältester, killed it. Now I'm going to pitch a tent for the night with Ella and Irča.

Thursday, August 26, 1943

It's terrible here now. There is a great deal of tension among the older, sensible children. They are going to send transports to a new ghetto—into the unknown.

And something else, 1,500 children will arrive tonight. They are from Poland. We are making toys and little bags and nets for them, etc.

I have diarrhea. Of 27 children, 19 have diarrhea and 16 are sick in bed. Two toilets for 100 children aren't enough, when there is infectious diarrhea in every 'Heim'.

What those toilets look like!!!

Friday, August 27, 1943

The children came at three this morning. They are full of lice. They only have what they are wearing. We are collecting things for them.

Saturday, September 4, 1943

Tomorrow they load the transport. From our room only Zdeňka is going so far. They are sending them in several batches. Zdeňka is acting very bravely.

Sunday, September 5, 1943

This was a day, but it's all over now. They are already in the 'šlojska.' From our room Pavla, Helena, Zdeňka, Olila and Popinka are going.

Everyone gave Zdeňka something, she's such a poor thing. I gave a half loaf of bread, a can of meat paste, linden tea and sugar. Her father came to pack her things and Zdeňka gave him bread, sugar and a tomato. He didn't want to take it, but we made him and said that we would bring Zdeňka some more food. He wept and thanked the children and the assistants for the care they had given Zdeňka. We all cried. Her father, mother, and brother didn't even have a bit of bread. We fixed them up so that from having nothing they had in a little while a full little suitcase and a small bag full of food.

At six in the evening they reported for the transport. Each one somewhere else. The parting was hard. After eight in the evening I went to look for Zdeňka. She was sitting on her luggage and she cried and laughed at the same time, she was so happy to see someone before she left. I slept all night, but I had terrible dreams and had rings under my eyes in the morning.

Monday, September 6, 1943

I got up at six to see Zdeňka again. When I came up to the Hamburg barracks the last people were just going through the back gates and getting on the train.

Everything was boarded up all around so no one could get to them and so they could not run away. I jumped over, ran up to the last people going through the gates. I saw the train pulling away and in one of the cars Zdeňka was riding away.

Mary Berg
(pseudonym)

15 YEARS OLD

POLAND

*M*ary Berg, a girl with American citizenship, was living in Poland with her parents at the beginning of the Nazi occupation. A year later, she was imprisoned in the Warsaw Ghetto despite the fact that her mother was not a Jew and was, in fact, an American.

In the ghetto, Mary witnessed and wrote of such horrors that it is almost inconceivable that she could have kept her sanity. But she never stopped recording what the Nazis did to her family, her friends, and her neighbors. Finally, she was informed that she and her mother were to be exchanged for German prisoners and that they would be released from Nazi custody.

Mary Berg's diary is a detailed eyewitness record of the atrocities committed in the Warsaw Ghetto. Because the Nazis had searched and looted every inch of the compound for three years, they didn't bother to search Mary when she was released. She was able to smuggle her huge diary out of the Warsaw Ghetto right under the noses of the Third Reich.

After being interned with other American citizens for a time in France, Mary and her family eventually were allowed to go to America, where she translated the diary from Polish into English and made arrangements to have it published when she was twenty years old. Only a few libraries in the world contain Mary's diary, which is called

Warsaw Ghetto: A Diary. *It was published in New York by L.B. Fischer Publishing Corporation in 1945.*

October 10, 1939

Today I am fifteen years old. I feel very old and lonely, although my family did all they could to make this day a real birthday. They even baked a macaroon cake in my honor, which is a great luxury these days. My father ventured out into the street and returned with a bouquet of Alpine violets. When I saw it I could not help crying.

I have not written my diary for such a long time that I wonder if I shall ever catch up with all that has happened. This is a good moment to resume it. I spend most of my time at home. Everyone is afraid to go out. The Germans are here.

I can hardly believe that only six weeks ago my family and I were at the lovely health resort of Ciechocinek, enjoying a carefree vacation with thousands of other visitors. I had no idea then what was in store for us. I got the first inkling of our future fate on the night of August 29 when the raucous blare of the giant loudspeaker announcing the latest news stopped the crowds of strollers in the streets. The word "war" was repeated in every sentence. Yet most people refused to believe that the danger was real, and the expression of alarm faded on their faces as the voice of the loudspeaker died away.

My father felt differently. He decided that we must return to our home in Lodz. In almost no time our valises stood packed and ready in the middle of the room. Little did we realize that this was only the beginning of several weeks of constant moving about from one place to another.

We caught the last train which took civilian passengers to Lodz. When we arrived we found the city in a state of confusion. A few days later it was the target of severe German bombardments.

We spent most of our time in the cellar of our house. When word came that the Germans had broken through the Polish front lines and were nearing Lodz, panic seized the whole population. At eleven o'clock at night crowds began to stream out of the city in different directions. Less than a week after our arrival from Ciechocinek we packed our necessities and set out once more.

Up to the very gates of the city we were uncertain which direction we should take—toward Warsaw or Brzeziny? Finally, along with most of the other Jews of Lodz, we took the road to Warsaw. Later we learned that the refugees who followed the Polish armies retreating in the direction of Brzeziny had been massacred almost to a man by German planes. . . .

When we arrived in Lowicz, the city was one huge conflagration. Burning pieces of wood fell on the heads of the refugees as they forced their way through the streets. Fallen telephone poles barred our path. The sidewalks were cluttered with furniture. Many people were burned in the terrible flames. The odor of scorched human flesh pursued us long after we had left the city.

By September 9 the supply of food we had taken from home was used up. There was nothing whatever to be had along the way. Weak from hunger, my mother fainted on the road. I dropped beside her, sobbing wildly, but she showed no sign of life. In a daze, my father ran ahead to find some water, while my younger sister stood stock-still, as if paralyzed. But it was only a passing spell of weakness.

In Sochaczew we managed to get a few sour pickles and some chocolate cookies that tasted like soap. This was all we had to eat the entire day. Finding a drink of water was almost as difficult as procuring food. All the wells along the way were dried up. Once we found a well filled with murky water, but the villagers warned us not to drink from it because they were sure it had been poisoned by German agents. We hurried on in spite of our parched lips and aching throats. . . .

We had our first taste of cooked food in Okecie, a suburb of Warsaw. A few soldiers in a deserted building shared their potato soup with us. After four days and nights of seemingly endless traveling we realized for the first time how tired we were. But we had to go on. . . .

In Warsaw we found women standing at the doorways of the houses, handing out tea and bread to the refugees who streamed into the capital in unending lines. And as tens of thousands of provincials entered Warsaw in the hope of finding shelter there, thousands of old-time residents of the capital fled to the country.

Relatives in the heart of Warsaw's Jewish quarter gave us a warm and hearty welcome, but constant air attacks drove us to the cellar during most of our stay with them. By September 12 the Germans began to destroy the center of the city. Once again we had to move, this time to seek better protection against the bombs.

The days that followed brought hunger, death, and

panic to our people. We could neither eat nor sleep. At first, in a new home on Zielna Street, we knew real comfort. The owners had fled the city, leaving a clean apartment for our use. There was even a maid to give us hot tea, and for the first time since our flight from Lodz we ate a real meal served on a table covered with a white cloth. It included herring, tomatoes, butter, and white bread. To get this bread my father had to stand for hours on a long line in front of a bakery. As he waited there, several German planes suddenly swooped down and strafed the people with machine guns. Instantly the line in front of the bakery dispersed, but one man remained. Disregarding the firing, my father took his place behind him. A moment later the man was hit in the head by a bullet. The entrance to the bakery shop was now free and my father made his purchase. . . .

I shall never forget September 23, the date of the Day of Atonement in 1939. The Germans deliberately chose that sacred Jewish holiday for an intensive bombardment of the Jewish district. In the midst of this bombardment a strange meteorological phenomenon took place: heavy snow mixed with hail began to fall in the middle of a bright, sunny day. For a while the bombing was interrupted, and the Jews interpreted the snow as a special act of heavenly intervention: even the oldest among them were unable to recall a similar occurrence. But later in the day the enemy made up for lost time with renewed fury. . . .

That night hundreds of buildings blazed all over the city. Thousands of people were buried alive in the ruins. But ten hours of murderous shelling could not break the resistance of Warsaw. Our people fought with increased stubbornness; even after the government had fled and Marshal Rydz-Smigly had abandoned his troops, men and women, young and old, helped in the defense of the capital. Those who were unarmed dug trenches; young girls organized first-aid squads in the doorways of the houses; Jews and Christians stood shoulder to shoulder and fought for their native land.

On the last night of the siege we sat huddled in a corner of the restaurant below our house. . . . We realized that our shelter was a firetrap, so we set out for Kozla Street to find safer quarters with our relatives, stumbling over the mutilated bodies of soldiers and civilians as we walked. We found only the skeleton of a house rising above a huge cellar packed full of people lying on the concrete floor. Somehow or other they made room for us. Beside me lay a little boy convulsed with pain from a wound. When his mother changed his dressing, one could see that a shell fragment was still embedded in his flesh and that gangrene had already set in. A little further on lay a woman whose foot had been torn off by a bomb. No medical aid was available for these people. The stench was unbearable. The corners were crowded with children wailing piteously. The grownups simply sat or lay motionless, with stony faces and vacant eyes. Hours went by. When daybreak came I was struck by the sudden stillness. My ears, accustomed to the crash of unceasing explosions, began to hum. It was the terrifying silence that precedes a great calamity, but I could not imagine anything worse than what we had already been through. Suddenly someone rushed into the cellar with the news that Warsaw had capitulated. No one stirred, but

I noticed tears in the eyes of the grownups. I, too, felt them choking in my throat, but my eyes were dry. So all our sacrifices had been in vain. Twenty-seven days after the outbreak of the war, Warsaw, which had held out longer than any other city in Poland, had been forced to surrender. . . .

We returned to our own street. On the pavement lay the carcasses of fallen horses from which people were carving pieces of meat. Some of the horses were still twitching, but the hungry wretches did not notice that; they were cutting the beasts up alive. We found the last place in which we had stayed, our apartment on the Nalewki, intact except for broken window panes. But there was nothing to eat. The janitor invited us to join him in a dinner of duck and rice. Later I learned that this duck was the last swan our janitor had caught in the pond in Krasinski Park. In spite of the fact that this water was polluted by rotting bodies, we felt no ill effects from that strange meal. . . .

Lodz, October 15, 1939

. . . We have been here in Lodz for only two days, but we know now that it was a mistake to return here. The Nazis are beginning to intensify their acts of terrorism against the native population, especially the Jews. Last week they set fire to the great synagogue, the pride of the Lodz community. They forbade the Jews to remove the sacred books, and the "shames" or beadle who wanted to save the holy relics was locked up inside the temple and died in the flames. My mother cannot forgive herself for having persuaded my father to bring us back here.

Lodz, November 3, 1939

Almost every day our apartment is visited by German soldiers who, under various pretexts, rob us of our possessions. I feel as if I were in prison. Yet I cannot console myself by looking out of the window, for when I peer from behind the curtain I witness hideous incidents like that which I saw yesterday:

A man with markedly Semitic features was standing quietly on the sidewalk near the curb. A uniformed German approached him and apparently gave him an unreasonable order, for I could see that the poor fellow tried to explain something with an embarrassed expression. Then a few other uniformed Germans came upon the scene and began to beat their victim with rubber truncheons. They called a cab and tried to push him into it, but he resisted vigorously. The Germans then tied his legs together with a rope, attached the end of the rope to the cab from behind, and ordered the driver to start. The unfortunate man's face struck the sharp stones of the pavement, dyeing them red with blood. Then the cab vanished down the street.

April 28, 1940

We have managed to obtain a separate apartment in the same house where we had been sharing rooms. My mother has tacked up her visiting card on the door, with the inscription: "American citizen." This inscription is a wonderful talisman against the German bandits who freely visit all Jewish apartments. As soon as German uniforms come into view at the outer door of our building, our neighbors come begging us to let them in so that they too can benefit from our miracu-

lous sign. Our two little rooms are filled to the brim—
for how could we refuse anyone? All of the neighbors
tremble with fear, and with a silent prayer on their lips
gaze at the two small American flags on the wall.

Jews who possess passports of neutral countries are
not compelled to wear arm bands or to do slave labor.
No wonder many Jews try to obtain such documents;
but not all have the means to buy them or the courage
to use them. Two of my friends have acquired papers
proving that they are nationals of a South American
republic. Thanks to these they can circulate freely in
the city. They went boldly to the Gestapo headquarters
at the Bruehl Palace to have these papers sealed with a
swastika; and the German experts did not realize that
they were forged. They can even go to the country to
buy food. . . .

November 15, 1940 [Warsaw]

Today the Jewish ghetto was officially established.
Jews are forbidden to move outside the boundaries
formed by certain streets. . . .

Work on the walls—which will be three yards
high—has already begun. Jewish masons, supervised
by Nazi soldiers, are laying bricks upon bricks. Those
who do not work fast enough are lashed by the over-
seers. It makes me think of the Biblical description of
our slavery in Egypt. But where is the Moses who will
release us from our new bondage? . . .

January 4, 1941

The ghetto is covered with deep snow. The cold is
terrible and none of the apartments are heated. Wher-

ever I go I find people wrapped up in blankets or huddling under feather beds, that is, if the Germans have not yet taken all these warm things for their own soldiers. The bitter cold makes the Nazi beasts who stand guard near the ghetto entrances even more savage than usual. Just to warm up as they lurch back and forth in the deep snow, they open fire every so often and there are many victims among the passers-by. Other guards who are bored with their duty at the gates arrange entertainments for themselves. For instance, they choose a victim from among the people who chance to go by, order him to throw himself in the snow with his face down, and if he is a Jew who wears a beard, they tear it off together with the skin until the snow is red with blood. When such a Nazi is in a bad mood, his victim may be a Jewish policeman who stands guard with him. . . .

Snow is falling slowly, and the frost draws marvelous flower patterns on the windowpanes. I dream of a sled gliding over the ice, of freedom. Shall I ever be free again? I have become really selfish. For the time being I am still warm and have food, but all around me there is so much misery and starvation that I am beginning to be very unhappy.

June 12, 1941

The ghetto is becoming more and more crowded; there is a constant stream of new refugees. These are Jews from the provinces who have been robbed of all their possessions. Upon their arrival the scene is always the same: the guard at the gate checks the identity of the refugee, and when he finds out that he is a Jew, gives him a push with the butt of his rifle as a sign that he may enter our Paradise. . . .

These people are ragged and barefoot, with the tragic eyes of those who are starving. Most of them are women and children. They become charges of the community, which sets them up in so-called homes. There they die sooner or later.

I have visited such a refugee home. It is a desolate building. The former walls of the separate rooms have been broken down to form large halls; there are no conveniences; the plumbing has been destroyed. Near the walls are cots made of boards and covered with rags. Here and there lies a dirty red feather bed. On the floor I saw half-naked, unwashed children lying listlessly. In one corner an exquisite little girl of four or five sat crying. I could not refrain from stroking her disheveled blond hair. The child looked at me with her big blue eyes, and said: "I'm hungry."

I was overcome by a feeling of utter shame. I had eaten that day, but I did not have a piece of bread to give to that child. I did not dare look in her eyes, and went away. . . .

Mortality is increasing. Starvation alone kills from forty to fifty persons a day. But there are always hundreds of new refugees to take their places. The community is helpless. All the hotels are packed, and hygienic conditions are of the worst. Soap is unobtainable; what is distributed as soap on our ration cards is a gluey mass that falls to pieces the moment it comes into contact with water. It makes one dirty instead of clean.

June 26, 1941

I am writing this in the bomb shelter of our house. I am on night duty, as a member of the home air defense. The Russians are bombing more and more frequently. We are situated in a dangerous spot, close to the main railway station. It is now eleven o'clock. I am sitting near a small carbide lamp. This is the first time since the opening of hostilities between Russia and Germany that I have been able to write. The shock was tremendous. War between Germany and Russia! Who could have hoped it would come so soon!

July 29, 1941

The typhus epidemic is raging. Yesterday the number of deaths from this disease exceeded two hundred. The doctors are simply throwing up their hands in despair. There are no medicines, and all the hospitals are overcrowded. . . .

September 20, 1941

The Nazis are victorious. Kiev has fallen. Soon Himmler will be in Moscow. London is suffering severe bombardments. Will the Germans win this war? No, a thousand times no! Why do not the Allies bomb German cities? Why is Berlin still intact? Germany must be wiped off the face of the earth. Such a people should not be allowed to exist. Not only are the uniformed Nazis criminals, but all the Germans, the whole civilian population, which enjoys the fruits of the looting and murders committed by their husbands and fathers.

September 23, 1941

Alas, our apprehensions before the holidays were justified. Only yesterday, on the eve of Rosh Hashana, the Germans summoned the community representatives with Engineer Czerniakow at their head and demanded that they deliver at once five thousand men for the labor camps. The community reused to obey this order. The Germans then broke into the ghetto and organized a real pogrom. The manhunt went on throughout yesterday and this morning, and shooting could be heard from all sides.

I happened to be in the street when the hunt began. I managed to rush into a doorway which was jammed with people, and I waited there for two hours. At a quarter past eight, considering that it takes half an hour to walk from Leszno Street to Sienna Street, I decided to go home in order to arrive before nine, the curfew hour, after which it is forbidden to be in the streets.

At the corner of Leszno and Zelazna Streets, an enormous mass of people stood drawn up in military ranks in front of the labor office. Most of them were young men between eighteen and twenty-five. The Jewish police were forced to see to it that no one ran away. These young men stood with lowered heads as though about to be slaughtered. And actually their prospects are not much better than slaughter. The thousands of men who have been sent to the labor camps thus far have vanished without leaving a trace.

Suddenly the door of a stationery store near which I stood, as if petrified, staring at the group of condemned men, opened, and I felt a hand on my shoulder. It was a Jewish policeman, who quickly dragged me inside.

A moment later, on the very spot where I had been standing, a man fell, struck by a bullet. . . .

Trembling, I looked at my watch. The curfew hour,

the hour of sure death on the ghetto streets, was approaching. Instinctively, I moved toward the exit. But the policeman would not let me go. When I told him how far I lived and that I did not care whether I was shot now or later, he promised to take me home.

I left the store with a few other people who wanted to get home. It was five minutes to nine. The policeman brought me to our doorway, and when I entered our apartment it was thirty minutes past curfew time. My parents had almost given me up for dead and flooded me with a hail of questions. But I was in no condition to answer them, and fell at once on my bed. Even now, as I write these lines, I am still shaken by my experience and I see before me the thousands of young Jews standing like sheep before a slaughterhouse. . . .

In a few months the mothers, wives, and sisters of these men will receive official postcards informing them that number such-and-such has died. It is inconceivable that we have the strength to live through it. The Germans are surprised that the Jews in the ghetto do not commit mass suicide, as was the case in Austria after the *Anschluss*. We, too, are surprised that we have managed to endure all these torments. This is the miracle of the ghetto.

The epidemic is taking a terrible toll. Recently the mortality reached five hundred a day. The home of every person who falls ill with typhus is disinfected. The apartments or rooms of those who die of it are practically flooded with disinfectants. The health department of the community is doing everything in its power to fight the epidemic, but the shortage of medicines and hospital space remains the chief cause of the huge mortality, and the Nazis are making it increasingly difficult to organize medical help. There is a widespread belief that the Nazis deliberately contaminated the ghetto with typhus bacilli in order to test methods of bacteriological warfare which they intend to apply against England and Russia. . . .

Few people today are earning their living by doing normal work. Real money can be made only in dishonest deals, but not many people engage in them; most Jews choose to go hungry rather than become tools in the hands of the Nazis.

But sometimes people are compelled to accept this role. If a person is caught committing a minor violation of the laws, such as wearing the arm band in a manner slightly different from that prescribed, he is arrested and tortured. Such a person is often anxious to commit suicide, but has no easy way of doing it. The Germans find their victims among these tortured people whose spirit and body are broken, and confront them with the choice of life or death. Such people lose all power of resistance; they agree to anything, and thus automatically become tools of the Gestapo. Their chief function is informing. The Nazis want to know who owns jewelry or foreign exchange. An informer can never get out of the Nazis' clutches; he must "accomplish" something to pay for the favor of being allowed to live and receive food. And the Nazis keep threatening him with the renewal of the same tortures.

Even these sad conditions give rise to various bits of gossip and jokes among us, and serve as material for songs and skits that are sung and played in cafés and theaters.

Every day at the Art Café on Leszno Street one can

hear songs and satires on the police, the ambulance service, the rickshas [hand trucks], and even the Gestapo, in a veiled fashion. The typhus epidemic itself is the subject of jokes. It is laughter through tears, but it is laughter. This is our only weapon in the ghetto—our people laugh at death and at the Nazi decrees. Humor is the only thing the Nazis cannot understand.

November 22, 1941

Outside, a blizzard is raging and the frost paints designs on the windowpanes. During these terribly cold days, one name is on everyone's lips: Kramsztyk, the man who presides over the distribution of fuel. Alas, the amount of coal and wood the Germans have assigned to the ghetto is so small that it is barely sufficient to heat the official buildings, such as the community administration, the post office, the hospitals, and the schools, so that almost nothing is left for the population at large. On the black market, coal fetches fantastic prices and often cannot be obtained at all.

In the streets, frozen human corpses are an increasingly frequent sight. On Leszno Street in front of the court building, many mothers often sit with children wrapped in rags from which protrude red frostbitten little feet. Sometimes a mother cuddles a child frozen to death, and tries to warm the inanimate little body. Sometimes a child huddles against his mother, thinking that she is asleep and trying to awaken her, while, in fact, she is dead. . . .

Hunger is assuming more and more terrible forms. The prices of foodstuffs are going up. . . .

It is not easy to walk in the street with a parcel in one's hand. When a hungry person sees someone with a parcel that looks like food, he follows him and, at an opportune moment, snatches it away, opens it quickly, and proceeds to satisfy his hunger. If the parcel does not contain food, he throws it away. No, these are not thieves; they are just people crazed by hunger.

The Jewish police cannot cope with them. And, indeed, who would have the heart to prosecute such unfortunates? . . .

December 9, 1941

America's entry into the war has inspired the hundreds of thousands of dejected Jews in the ghetto with a new breath of hope. The Nazi guards at the gates have long faces. Some are considerably less insolent, but on others the effect has been exactly opposite and they are more unbearable than ever. Most people believe that the war will not last long now and that the Allies' victory is certain.

February 27, 1942

Shootings have now become very frequent at the ghetto exits. Usually they are perpetrated by some guard who wants to amuse himself. Every day, morning and afternoon, when I go to school, I am not sure whether I will return alive. I have to go past two of the most dangerous German sentry posts: at the corner of Zelazna and Chlodna Streets near the bridge, and at the corner of Krochmalna and Grzybowska Streets. At the latter place there is usually a guard who has been nicknamed "Frankenstein," because of his notorious

cruelty. Apparently this soldier cannot go to sleep unless he has a few victims to his credit; he is a real sadist. When I see him from a distance I shudder. He
looks like an ape: small and stocky, with a swarthy
grimacing face. This morning, on my way to school,
as I was approaching the corner of Krochmalna and
Grzybowska Streets, I saw his familiar figure, torturing
some ricksha driver whose vehicle had passed an inch
closer to the exit than the regulations permitted. The
unfortunate man lay on the curb in a puddle of blood.
A yellowish liquid dripped from his mouth to the pavement. Soon I realized that he was dead, another victim
of the German sadist. The blood was so horribly red
the sight of it completely shattered me.

April 28, 1942

Last night sixty more persons were executed. They
were members of the underground, most of them well-
to-do people who financed the secret bulletins. Many
printers who were suspected of helping to publish the
underground papers were also killed. Once again in
the morning there were corpses in the streets. . . .

In our garden everything is green. The young onions are shooting up. We have eaten our first radishes.
The tomato plants spread proudly in the sun. The
weather is magnificent. The greens and the sun remind
us of the beauty of nature that we are forbidden to
enjoy. A little garden like ours is therefore very dear to
us. The spring this year is extraordinary. A little lilac
bush under our window is in full bloom.

May 4, 1942

On the "Aryan" side the population celebrated May
1 and May 3 by a complete boycott of the Nazis.

Throughout those days the people tried to avoid taking trolley cars or buying newspapers, for the money goes straight to the Germans. Someone put a wreath of flowers on the tomb of the Unknown Soldier. The people deliberately stayed at home, so that a dead silence prevailed in the city. In the ghetto, too, the mood was somehow different. Although many Poles, poisoned by anti-Semitism, deny that their brothers of the Jewish faith are their co-citizens, the Jews, despite the inhuman treatment to which they are subjected, show their patriotism in every possible way. Recently there has been much talk of the partisan groups fighting in the woods of the Lublin region; there are many Jews among them, who fight like all the others for a common goal. And yet the Polish anti-Semites say, "It's a good thing, let the Jews sit behind their walls. At last Poland will be Jewless." . . .

It is beginning to be hot, and often, instead of going to school, I take a blanket and a pillow and go to our roof to sunbathe. This practice is widespread in the ghetto; the houses with flat roofs have been transformed into city beaches.

At 20 Chlodna Street the charge for entering the terracelike roof is one zloty fifty groszy. There are folding chairs, cool drinks, and a bird's-eye view of Warsaw. On our own roof I am always alone. It is pleasant to lie there in the sun, where I can see the quarter beyond the wall. The white spires of a church are very near me. They are surrounded by linden branches and the perfume of these lovely trees reaches as far as my roof. Further on there are private houses now used as German barracks. The air is pure here, and I think of the wide world, of distant lands, of freedom.

July 5, 1942

Fewer and fewer students come to our school; now they are afraid to walk in the streets. . . . A few days ago I, too, ceased completely attending school.

Today I boldly removed my arm band. After all, officially I am now an American citizen.

The inhabitants of the street looked at me with curiosity: "That's the girl who is going to America." In this street everyone knows everyone else. Every few minutes people approached me and asked me to note the addresses of their American relatives, and to tell them to do everything possible for their unfortunate kin.

August, 1942

Behind the Pawiak gate we are experiencing all the terror that is abroad in the ghetto. For the last few nights we have been unable to sleep. The noise of the shooting, the cries of despair, are driving us crazy. I have to summon all my strength to write these notes. I have lost count of the days, and I do not know what day it is. But what does it matter? We are here as on a little island amidst an ocean of blood. The whole ghetto is drowning in blood. We literally see fresh human blood, we can smell it. Does the outside world know anything about it? Why does no one come to our aid? I cannot go on living; my strength is exhausted. How long are we going to be kept here to witness all this? . . .

During the last two weeks more than 100,000 people have been deported from the ghetto. The number of those murdered is also very large. Everyone who can is trying to get a job in the German factories of

Toebens, Schultz, and Hallmann. Fantastic sums are paid for a labor card.

September 20, 1942

The massacres have aroused the underground leaders to greater resistance. The illegal papers are multiplying and some of them reach us even here in the Pawiak. They are full of good reports from the battle fronts. The Allies are victorious in Egypt, and the Russians are pushing the enemy back at Moscow. The sheets explain the meaning of the deportations and tell of the fate of the deported Jews. The population is summoned to resist with weapons in their hands, and warned against defeatist moods, and against the idea that we are completely helpless before the Nazis. "Let us die like men and not like sheep," ends one proclamation in a paper called *To Arms!* . . .

October 10, 1942

Today is my birthday. I spent all day on my mattress. Everyone came to congratulate me, but I did not answer. At night my sister managed to snatch three turnips, and we had a real feast to celebrate the occasion.

October 22, 1942

Is this really our last night in the Pawiak? Is it possible that tomorrow we shall leave? Before nightfall we arranged a "farewell dinner" in the men internees' room. We ate turnips, and our representative, Mr. S., made a speech to the twenty-one American citizens. On the table we placed two little American flags that I had kept in my suitcase, as a relic, since the beginning of the war. The mood was one of elation. Noemi W. wore a silk wrapper that looked like an elegant evening gown. She recited and sang songs. I, too, sang several English songs. The attendants watched us and I had the feeling that they envied us.

December 17, 1942

Dita W., one of yesterday's arrivals, told us last night what she had heard about the camp at Treblinki. During her frequent visits to Gestapo headquarters at Aleja Szucha she became acquainted with a German who was an official in this death camp. He did not realize that she was Jewish, and told her with great satisfaction how the deported Jews were being murdered there, assuring her that the Germans would finally "finish off" all the Jews. . . .

The actual death house of Treblinki is situated in a thick wood. The people are taken in trucks to buildings where they are ordered to undress completely. Each is given a cake of soap and told that he must bathe before going to the labor camp. The naked people, men, women, and children separately, are led into a bathhouse with a slippery tile floor. They tumble down the moment they enter it. Each small compartment is so filled with people that again they must lie on top of one another. After the bathhouse is entirely filled, strongly concentrated hot steam is let in through the windows. After a few minutes the people begin to choke in horrible pain.

After the execution the dead bodies are carried out by Jews—the youngest and most vigorous are especially chosen by the Nazis for this purpose. Other Jews are compelled to sort out the shoes and clothes of the victims. After each transport the Jews employed to bury the dead or sort their belongings are relieved by others. They are unable to stand this work for more than a week. Most of them lose their minds and are shot. Even the Ukrainian and German personnel are often relieved, because the older German soldiers begin to complain of their tasks. Only the chief German authorities remain the same.

Escape from Treblinki is impossible, yet two young Jews managed to do the impossible. After long wanderings in the woods they arrived in Warsaw and related other details. According to them the Germans employ various gases as well as electricity in certain execution chambers. Because of the enormous number of the murdered, the Germans have constructed a special machine to dig graves.

People who have traveled in trains past Treblinki say that the stench there is so poisonous that they must stop up their nostrils.

After Dita's accounts none of us could sleep.

December 26, 1942

It looks as though our departure is really imminent. The Nazis are making great efforts to impress us favorably. The day before Christmas all the internees' quarters were scrubbed, even the rooms occupied by the Jews. On Christmas Day we had an exceptionally good meal which consisted of a thick pea soup, a portion of sauerkraut, potatoes, and two pounds of bread.

At nine in the evening Commissioner Nikolaus, accompanied by his aides Jopke and Fleck, and three SS men in uniform, entered our room, saluted us, and assured us that we would surely leave in the very near future.

This morning we received a visit from the hangman, Bürckel. He wore his gala uniform and, probably on account of the holiday, did not carry his riding crop. He had had a good dose of liquor and was in an exuberant mood. He approached old Rabbi R., took him by the hand and, shaking with laughter, wished him a Merry Christmas. "We Germans can be kind, too!" he snickered as he staggered out of our room.

January 1, 1943

New Year's Eve for me was full of nightmares. I fell asleep and woke up several times, for I was tormented by horrible dreams; I relived all the scenes I had witnessed during these years of war. . . . Then I was awakened by shouts and laughter coming from the direction of the prison yard. The Nazi officials were gaily welcoming the New Year. From time to time I heard the sound of shots, followed again by laughter and the noise of broken glass. Then came roaring drunken voices.

The first day of 1943 is cloudy and snowy. As I write these lines I cannot stop thinking of Dita W.'s stories of Treblinki. I see before me the tiled bathhouses filled with naked people choking in the hot steam. How many of my relatives and friends have perished there? How many young, still unlived lives? I curse the coming of the New Year.

February 27, 1944

At last a date has been set! The exchange will take place in Lisbon on March 5. Wounded American soldiers and civilian internees are scheduled for exchange. But it is no clear yet what the ratio of the exchange will be: five Germans for one American, or vice versa, five Americans for one German. Various rumors are circulating on the subject. The camp administration organizes a new registration every hour; new people are put on the lists, old ones are crossed off. We are all at a terrible pitch of tension and nervousness. Our family was on the first two lists, but now we have been taken off them. My mother is rushing around from one office to another. Only about thirty persons are supposed to go with the first batch, while there are one hundred and fifty candidates for exchange in Vittel. All these shifts and rumors have completely shattered our nerves.

March 3, 1944

A few minutes ago we exchanged all our money for dollars. This has finally reassured us; we really believe we are going to America now. All the men were made to sign a pledge that they would not fight against Germany in any army. When they left the cars to sign this pledge we saw a train with German internees arrive on another track. They have come from America to be exchanged for us. All of us actually pitied these Germans.

March 4, 1944

Our train is now on Spanish territory. At the stations some people greet us with the "V" sign. The poverty of Spain strikes one at once. Ragged children stretch out their hands, begging for a coin. There are many soldiers, especially smartly dressed officers. The civilian population is dressed in rags, and the people have hollow cheeks.

Many of the Germans who escorted us have remained on the French side of the border, and those who still accompany us now are dressed in mufti. With their uniforms they have shed their insolence.

March 5, 1944

We have just crossed the Portuguese border. The uniformed Spanish police have been replaced by Portuguese secret police. We are still in the same train. Here, too, people greet us with "V" signs.

Our train is approaching Lisbon. I can see the sails of various ships. Someone in our car has just shouted the word: "Gripsholm!" This unfamiliar Swedish word means freedom to us.

I was awakened by the sound of the ship's engine. The "Gripsholm" was on the open sea. I went out on deck and breathed in the endless blueness. The blood-drenched earth of Europe was far behind me. The feeling of freedom almost took my breath away. . . .

On deck I made friends with American soldiers and fliers who had been shot down on missions over Germany, and who had been exchanged together with us. Some of them had empty hanging sleeves. Others walked on crutches. Two young officers had horribly disfigured faces; others had had their faces burned. One of them had lost both legs, but a smile never left his lips.

I felt close to these Americans, and when I told them about what the Nazis had done in the ghetto they understood me. . . .

By nightfall of March 14 the outline of the American coast began to emerge from the mist. The passengers went out on deck and lined the railings. I was reminded of the Biblical story of the flood, and of Noah's ark, when it finally reached dry land.

All that day I felt completely broken, as though I had to bear the burden of many, many years. I did not take part in the entertainment that night. I lay in a corner of the deck, listening to the sound of the waves that were growing stormier and stormier.

On March 15 our ship approached New York. People who had gone through years of common misfortune began to say farewell to each other. A mood of fraternal affection prevailed among us. On everyone's face there was an expression of restless expectation.

I saw the skyscrapers of New York, but my thoughts were in Warsaw . . .

I shall do everything I can to save those who can still be saved, and to avenge those who were so bitterly humiliated in their last moments. And those who were ground into ash, I shall always see them alive. I will tell, I will tell everything, about our sufferings and our struggles and the slaughter of our dearest, and I will demand punishment for the German murderers and their Gretchens in Berlin, Munich, and Nuremberg who enjoyed the fruits of murder, and are still wearing the clothes and shoes of our martyrized people.

Ina Konstantinova

RUSSIA

*B*efore Nazi Germany attacked the Soviet Union, sixteen-year-old Ina Konstantinova was living a quiet, comfortable life with her parents and younger sister, Renok, near the town of Kashin, northeast of Moscow. She had been keeping a diary for several years, mostly focusing on her moods, adolescent existential angst, and the close friendships she had with other girls and boys.

Then, the night before her sixteenth birthday, in July of 1940, she wrote a melancholy farewell to her childhood and spoke of death with a question as to whether she would ever reach old age. On June 22, 1941, Germany bombed Russia, beginning the war in which she would give her life, at age twenty, while serving as a partisan.

From the time she first learned that Russia was under attack, Ina wanted to serve in the combat zone. This is not as unusual as it may seem since one million women served in the Soviet armed forces during World War II, the majority of them in active combat. But Ina chose the riskiest way of fighting the Nazis. She volunteered as a saboteur and spy in the partisan underground when she was only seventeen years old. This was commonly known to be so dangerous that Ina had to "elope" in order to leave her mother and father whom she thought might try to prevent her from going.

Formerly given to moodiness and restlessness, Ina

seemed to find new meaning and purpose in her life with the partisan movement. She was never happier than when she was swathed in ammunition belts and carrying a submachine gun. Even the deaths of many of her comrades did not dissuade her from proceeding with her mission to kill as many Nazis as possible.

What follows is a selection of Ina's diary entries and her letters home to her family. Many of the letters are undated and are intentionally vague about her whereabouts. What is known for certain is that on March 4, 1944, the dugout in which Ina and her platoon of partisan scouts were hiding was surrounded by a detachment of German soldiers. When she realized that she and her comrades were trapped, Ina ordered them to leave while she stayed behind to cover their retreat with submachine gunfire.

The next day, the partisans came back to the dugout and found Ina lying dead under a nearby pine tree. Her friends and fellow partisans buried her there and carved her initials into the tree. Her remains were later exhumed and transferred to a cemetery in her hometown of Kashin.

For a girl to die in Soviet partisan service was not unique. What caused Ina to be regarded as a national hero was her writing. Her parents were instrumental in having her diary and letters published by the Soviet government. From that time on, Ina was held up as an example for Soviet youth to follow.

These excerpts from Ina's diary and letters were taken from a translation by Kazimiera J. Cottam, Ph.D., published by New Military Publishing in 1988.

29 July 1940

ON THE LAST DAY OF MY CHILDHOOD

It is painful to give up all that is close and dear to us, especially one's childhood.

I know one thing: the pure, radiant joys—the joys of childhood—are gone forever. Good-bye, my morning. My day, bright but exhausting, has begun. And there, at the end, my old age awaits me. But will I reach it? Better not to experience this evening of life at all. For it brings . . . death.

Good-bye childhood . . . forever.

22 June 1941

Only yesterday everything was so peaceful, so quiet, and today . . . my God!

At noon we heard Molotov's speech broadcast over the radio: Germany is bombing our nation, and German bombs have fallen on Kiev, Zhitomir, and other Ukrainian cities. The country is endangered. I can't describe my state of mind as I was listening to this speech! I became so agitated that my heart seemed about to jump out. The country is mobilizing; could I continue as before? No! I ought to make myself useful to my Homeland, to the best of my ability, in its hour of need. We must win!

23 June 1941

This is the second day of the war. Only the second day, but these two days were more eventful than the past two years. Our region was placed under martial law. This means that on the streets, too, lights are forbidden after 10:00 p.m. General mobilization has been declared. Our boys have already been called up by the Military Commissariat; soon they will go away.

Papa has already been mobilized, too, but he is still in Kashin. And what about me? If only there was a way of making myself useful at the front! Immediately, without any hesitation, I would then volunteer for service in the combat zone. But . . . what can I do there now? Well, nothing. But my time will come, too.

3 July 1941

Oh, what a night we had today! I'll never, never forget it. I'll start at the beginning. A week ago, I joined a voluntary aid detachment. We train every day from seven to ten. Yesterday, some of us were summoned for duty to the District Committee of the Red Cross. The time was 10:30 p.m. We were issued night passes, bandages, respirators, and medical bags. Then we were sent to the Technical School. Here everything was made ready to receive a trainload of wounded soldiers. Covered trucks and buses stood by; we climbed into them. I found myself among the Technical School kids.

We sat up all night, until 4:00 a.m. Finally, we drove to the train station. The train arrived at 5:30 a.m., and the unloading began. What an experience! I'll never forget the face of an agitated woman, accompanying the wounded, who—with tears in her eyes—almost threw her arms around my neck and kept repeating joyfully: "My dear little sister, have we really arrived? It is so good to see you!"

I'll never forget the blue eyes of a soldier, a mere youngster, semi-closed and suddenly opening up and flashing from an unbearable pain. How he suffered! I'll never forget this dark-haired youth with both legs torn off.

We carried, transported, and guided people. . . . But what I remember best was the mood of the soldiers.

They all believed in victory, all were cheerful. We transported a girl soldier, a Latvian, wounded in one leg. She spoke almost no Russian. There were many wounded civilians, too, mainly from Riga.

No, I could never fully describe what I lived through that night. I was completely tired out. But it didn't matter!

16 July 1941

A terrible misfortune has befallen this country. The Germans are already so near. . . . They are bombing Leningrad, Mozhaysk. They are advancing toward Moscow. . . .

We are training in a voluntary aid detachment, and are working in a hospital.

How troubled our life has become! There is an airfield near Kashin; aircraft take off from it constantly. Military detachments march along the streets. Field units, antiaircraft guns, and tanks have arrived.

Even the atmosphere has changed somehow. What does the future hold in store for us? I am anxious to finish training, and . . . to go to the front. I dream of . . . Nazi defeat, of defending our Homeland and making us happy again!

5 August 1941

On 30 July I turned seventeen. Did I foresee a year ago what is happening today? And what lies ahead for me a year from now? If the war has not yet ended by then, I'll definitely go to the front. They are bound to take me by then. Indeed, by then I would already be eighteen.

Every night Moscow is subjected to air raids. The enemy troops are coming closer and closer. How awful! But, never mind, they will soon be stopped.

17 December 1941

We heard good news over the radio again today. The Germans are receiving a sound beating and are on the run. Well, that's splendid! Soon we'll likely hear a communique from the Informburo to the effect that our troops have entered Berlin. What a holiday it would be! I can't wait!

8 April 1942

What luck: I am so glad, glad; I've never felt so good! Today I have been accepted for work behind German lines. I am in heaven! Oh, I am so happy! I'll write about everything, everything later on. I am so glad!

[Undated]

My dear ones, please forgive me!

I know—it was mean on my part to treat you as I did, but it's better this way: under no circumstances could I have withstood Mama's tears. Don't be too upset, don't feel sorry for me, because my fondest, long-standing wish has come true. I am happy! Remember this. Tomorrow, I'll give you all, all the details, and meanwhile I can only tell you that I am going to join a detachment. Papochka, forgive me in the name of everything that is holy, forgive me for what you call my deceiving you. I came to the Regional Committee . . . and it was too late to back out. My dearest and darling family, only don't you cry and feel sorry for me. After all, this is how I wish to live my life. This is how I visualize my happiness. Never mind! It'll be so good to see you, and to kiss you affectionately on my return in the fall.

Lots of love to you all,

Your disobedient Inka.

[Undated]

Hello, my darling Papusya and Mamochka!

Yesterday, we left Kalinin and spent the night here, the place from which I am writing now. We are having a wonderful trip. It is true that the weather is cool, but I've warm clothing at my disposal. Do you know that my superiors have even told Colonel-General Konev [the Front commander] about me, and I'll soon go to meet him, because he wished to see me?

I am flattered; shouldn't I be? Our partisan commanders want me to stay at their HQ; I would be completely safe there, but I don't want that. Well, all right, we'll see what happens when we get there, and in the meantime I am so well taken care of!

The commander gave me a personal weapon—a pistol with two clips—and in Toropets I am to receive a submachine gun (a German one), which I've already learned to use. On the whole, during these past few days I learned so many new things, so many interesting things, and I'll never forget this time of my life.

We passed through places destroyed and scarred by the Germans. Oh, what horrors I have seen! So much destruction, so many tragedies they have caused; we must repay them for all this! My dear ones, if you had seen all that I did, you too would have come with me to join the detachment. Such interesting work awaits me there! Oh, I am so happy!

Ina.

[Undated]

Hello, my dear ones!

I am writing this letter to you from the village of Kun'ya, where we arrived yesterday evening; this is the last day of my stay in Soviet-held land until I return after the victory. Tomorrow we'll cross over "there." Don't worry, I'll be completely safe.

I have found my niche; here I am among friends. I am at peace with myself, and I'll definitely return victorious, but should something happen to me—believe me, I'll die honorably. This is how we all feel. Already many hardships have to be endured, but you should see me, running about carrying out assignments; I have been detailed as the duty person, and I cook dinner, so that you wouldn't recognize me. I sleep very little; I am terribly sunburnt, my face is weatherbeaten and perhaps coarsened a bit, but it doesn't matter.

Besides, I eat very well. So I am not likely to lose any weight.

In short, "life is beautiful and wonderful!" Today the Germans carried out as many as four air raids against our village. The bombing was awful, and their machine guns gave us a good thrashing. The bombs exploded about 70 meters from us, and bullets whistled literally above our heads (I lay in a ditch). But you see—I survived. Consequently, nothing will ever happen to me;

I believe this wholeheartedly. From now on, for some time I won't be able to write to you directly, but don't worry; you'll be informed about me by a man who will keep in touch with you.

23 June 1942

I haven't written for a long time. So much has happened! I was not mistaken: this copy-book will see a great deal.

I particularly remember the events of 19 June. At night a large punitive detachment approached our village very, very close. The exchange of fire continued throughout the night. In the morning, when we woke up, villages burned all around us. Soon the first casualty was brought to me. My hands were covered with blood. Then I took this seriously wounded man to a doctor, 6 kilometers away. When I returned, we had to execute a certain village elder, a collaborator. We went to get him; we read him the sentence and led him to the place of execution. I felt awful.

In the evening, about eleven, just as I was getting ready to go to bed, another wounded man was brought in. Again I dressed his wounds, and again had to deliver him to a doctor. And the weather was terrible; it was cold, dark, raining, and windy! I dressed warm and we went. My sick man instantly froze; I had to give him at first my raincape and then my jacket. I had only a blouse on, and was terribly chilled. On the way, the cart broke down and I fixed it, and then we got lost. In short, it took us four hours to get to our destination. I barely had the time to warm up a bit when I had to start back. I returned in the morning; I had quite a night!

8 July 1942

Hello, my dear Papochka, Mamusen'ka, and Renok!

My life is unchanged, that is, I feel remarkably well. Only don't get the idea that I am saying this just to reassure you. No, in fact, I am very satisfied with my current life.

From the very first day I became a partisan I forgot what it's like to be in a bad mood. The minute I appear crestfallen, our commanders and girls begin to joke, laugh, and cheer me up; in no time I again feel well.

Actually we have fun all the time. Especially in the evenings, when the entire staff, the eight of us, gather at the home base. Everyone tells a story of some kind and makes jokes; we giggle and go to sleep very, very late. By and large, work and leisure leave us no time for moping.

28 July 1942

My dear ones, my darlings!

Well, so we are going away in a half hour. Everything, absolutely everything, has been gathered, checked, and prepared. If you could only see me now—with field service marching order! There are machine-gun belts around my waist and a carbine is slung over my shoulder. I am also carrying a kit-bag, cartridge pouches and grenades, and in my pockets I've a Walther and a field dressing. I am wearing a big, turtleneck wool sweater and a jacket; I find this outfit most comfortable. We are saying good-bye to our Kupuy, and to the dear places that we have become so accustomed to. We are saying good-bye to our native land. We are about to go behind enemy lines for two months. And then to you, home. Don't expect any more mail from me, unless something happens to me; only then you'll get a letter or, more accurately, a message will then be transmitted by radio to the Front HQ and the HQ, in turn, will communicate with you.

But this isn't likely to happen. I'll return soon, in one piece, alive and well.

[Undated]

Hello, my own dearest darlings!

I don't know how to begin. Well, all right; first of all, I am alive and well, and feel wonderful. It is only three days since I returned from behind German lines. Again, I had a bit of an experience. Again, I was caught. This time I fell straight into German clutches. I didn't expect it would all end so well, but, obviously, I returned unharmed. I've lived through so much. . . . Honestly, I thought I might go gray. I'll tell you everything when we meet. I am now detached from the Brigade, on our territory and among our people. I nearly went crazy with joy after I crossed the front line and when I saw our people!

In a few days, I'll probably go back "there."

Don't worry about me. I am deeply convinced that nothing will happen to me, and that I'll soon come home on leave. Probably, in a few days, I'll receive many, many letters from you. This would make me so happy!

I feel remarkably well. After all, I am a hundred times happier than all the girls back home—dancing and supposedly having fun—because during these difficult times I too am useful to my Homeland which needs me, and not for nothing I am a Soviet person. Even if I were to go hungry, fall into Nazi clutches, and walk barefooted hundreds of kilometers—still I would be very rich, for I've the sense of true satisfaction. Well, my dear ones, lots of love and kisses to you.

Your Ina.

24 August 1942

My darling Mamusen'ka!

A few days ago, I received the first letter from you.

If you only knew how infinitely happy I was! How I cried over it! As if the two and a half months during which I heard nothing from you didn't happen. You wrote it on 6 August.

I now lead the kind of life I dreamed of: a soldier's life—active and for real. It is true that I am awfully sorry it is coming to an end. That is, not my life, but this kind of life. I am doing quite well, apparently. The command appreciates my service: I have been serving in a reconnaissance platoon from the beginning, and am now an expert scout. I carry a submachine gun and a pistol, and I ride Mashka, a nice, fiery, little mare. In no respect am I inferior to the boys; in fact, on the contrary, the commander often singles me out as an example to follow.

My personal score now stands at fifteen Germans killed.

I'll soon go to Moscow to study. Consequently, it is not unlikely that we'll soon see each other.

Meanwhile, lots of love and kisses to you.

Your Ina.

Colin Perry

ENGLAND

*A*n eighteen-year-old office boy living with his parents and brother, Alan, in a suburb of London when the blitz began, Colin Perry set out to write a journal. As it was intended for no one other than himself, the words flowed rapidly, for they were no more than the tangible expression of what was going on in his mind and of the sights about him.

Colin wrote so much, that even though he kept his war diary only from March to November of 1940, there was still enough material to comprise a full-length book. Thirty-two years later, the Imperial War Museum in London wrote, "It is a minor classic of the psychology of adolescence," and encouraged him to have the work published, and his diary was published as Boy in the Blitz by London publisher Leo Cooper Ltd., in 1972.

By no means content to limit himself to portraits of his home life, Colin recklessly ignored air raid warnings as he bicycled through the streets of London gathering news for his diary. He barged across police lines and refused to take shelter even though commanded to by the wardens. Binoculars in one hand and his notebook in the other, Colin was ever at the ready to race his bicycle to the highest hill for close-up views of balloons, parachutists, and bombers.

Proclaiming that he never felt fear during any of his exploits, Colin seemed impervious to the emotional im-

pact of the war. He said he regarded it with "curiosity" and "indifference." However, after several months of nearly nightly bombings, he began to see that the war was a dreadful reality that was crushing the life out of his country and causing tremendous suffering for his friends and neighbors. When he was face-to-face with mangled bodies and death, Colin came to the conclusion that all the dog-fights—and the sweat, toil, and blood Churchill had warned of—did not equal glory. "A new Perry," as he called himself, began to feel compassion for the suffering people of London.

In November of 1940, Colin left off writing his diary when he was accepted by the Merchant Marine. He signed on as ship's writer aboard H.M.T. Strathallan and sailed from England for "destination unknown."

After the war, Colin Perry became a chartered certified accountant, married, and had two children. He is still living in England. His diary is available from the author in a self-published paperback edition.

London: Monday, 17 June, 1940

France has capitulated. Britain is alone.

Is it better to die, if die we must, as an Empire and foremost world power, fighting to the last drop of our blood, or now, immediately, lay down arms and not hold our country and breed in lunacy of death for the sake of tradition? If our Government realize the situation is hopeless, is it right that they should risk the appalling loss of life which must result if we pursue or struggle to end this Nazi tyranny? Condemn him to hell who is responsible for bringing Britain to the verge of her existence—Britain whom we love, and whom our ancestors placed into the leadership of the world.

12 July

Oh boy, oh boy, *Oh Boy!*

Just back from lunch and you can guess the reason for my jubilation. Or can you? Yep, you're right. It's the 'Girl in the ABC'—tra la lah la . . . I am full of the joys of Spring, tra lah.

We caught one another's eye . . . she looked, just dead straight ahead . . . at me (of course) and I—well I did the same as her. A glimmer of a smile flickered round her face.

There you are. The ice cracked slightly, ever so slight, and I can hardly wait until Monday lunch-time. We each appreciated the other's amusement, of that I am sure. Well now I do know, come hither go thither, I am resolved to speak to her—sooner, or later.

It was a tremendous sensation—her smile. It somehow warmed 'the cockles of my English heart,' and I hope I warmed hers, bless her heart. Tra lah lah . . .

17 July

Tonight we in our proud Island prepare ourselves for the word that the invader has commenced his attack. The air-raid wardens have passed information round that the Military at Tolworth will tonight throw up a smoke-screen, which will spread and envelop the whole Metropolis, blot out vital objectives, and generally throw invading hordes into confusion. At any moment—now, as I write this—the attack may commence. We are waiting with calm fortitude for the inevitable. Air-raids, massed murder, total devastation of beautiful buildings: the unknown: and gas, too, maybe, to poison our food and pollute our water. All these evil possibilities confront the people of England, now. We have witnessed countries torn to shreds by this Moloch of our age. We, alone, await his onslaught, calm, confident, determined.

Despite all this, which but a year ago would have sounded fantastic, my ordinary life continues. And today it is not the war which occupies the whole of my inner mind, but 'the Girl in the ABC.' I am callous about the war business. Certainly not in any degree scared or anxious. I am intensely interested. *Britain at Bay*, the film I have just seen, makes me want to join the army tomorrow. It showed our fair Kentish fields, the pleasant Surrey woodlands, the broad moors of Devon and Cornwall to the wild bracken of Scotland; from the smelly City to the remotest village hamlet— this is the 'front-line'; this is where we stand to defend our right with all our might. Somehow it is magnificent and terrible in one.

15 August (evening)

Overhead a hum of aircraft became audible, and I looked upwards into the slowly setting sun thinking to see a 'Security Patrol'; then I saw three whirling 'planes, and Alan yelled, 'Look! see them, it's a German!' and by God it was. I tore hell for leather to the top of our block of flats, and standing on the window-sill of the hall-landing I looked out over Surrey. Yes, thunder alive, there over Croydon were a pack of 'planes, so tiny and practically invisible in the haze, and—by God! the Hun was bombing Croydon Airport. I yelled down to Mother, roused the Court, 'Look, Croydon's being dive-bombed' and I rushed to commandeer my excellent vantage point. Machine-guns rattled over the still air, and there, only a few miles away bombs commenced to drop. At last, the war was here! At last I was seeing some excitement. Anti-aircraft guns threw a dark ring around the darting 'planes, Spitfires and Hurricanes roared to battle. A terrific cloud of smoke ascended from the town; two more fires, obviously slight, rose on the wind. Boy this was IT!

I munched an apple and went out armed with my enviable story. I didn't get far though, for a whine, fluctuating, grew from afar to a sudden deafening crescendo. Only the air-raid sirens. Hell, they were a bit behind time, the damn raid was over. Least I was convinced it was, and it happened I was proved right. Still people were not to know that, and all the milling throngs calmly drifted to their nearest shelter. The wail died away, and the roads, practically deserted, made way for a police car speeding along the Upper Tooting Road at something like 80 mph complete with a whirring, piercing siren. Just like G-men on the films, I thought. The wardens efficiently took up their action stations, and I, well I still sat munching my apple on the steps, thinking well at last a bit of excitement had hit the everyday routine. My one regret was I had to be an onlooker; boy, if only I had been in one of those Spitfires—oh Hell! those 'planes got me; I must be a pilot!

Well, I hardly imagined that my journal would ever bear such an interesting story. I would mention that I was absolutely the first person in the whole of our district to spot the raiders and definitely the first by far to witness the actual bombardment. Naturally, all the

papers will be hot on the trail. By God why on earth
didn't I phone to the *Express* an eye witness view of
the bombing? Hells bells I might have got my name in
the paper. Ah, well, it's too late now.

Sunday, 18 August

We had just settled down to a delightful dinner—
chicken, marrow, peas, new potatoes and baked potatoes, stuffing and gravy, when the air-raid sirens
started. Dad and Alan both took their dinners down
the shelter. I, only dressed in pants and singlet, took
some four minutes to dress, and hugging my brief case
I too toddled off down. Aircraft were roaring overhead,
and I didn't have time to survey the scene. However,
having deposited my belongings safely below ground,
I came up to the surface. I went across to No. 1 block
to the top floor, and sure enough Croydon once again
was in smoke. A big fire also showed in the Wimble-
don direction. Putney too appeared to have been hit,
but it may have been a factory chimney. As I was
looking out I heard a terrific roar approaching, and
being from the north I could not see anything from
where I stood, so I ran into the court, to the shelter,
where everyone was busily scanning the sky. Then I
shouted—first again—some 30 or 40 enemy bombers,
accompanied by fighters, were sweeping in a direct
line for Croydon. They were indeed very near us. It
presented an amazing spectacle, like a swarm of bees
surrounding their queen; fascinating, most certainly. A
puff of smoke and the sound of a gun signalled our
retreat down the shelter. I fancied I heard the whine of
dive-bombers, most assuredly we heard the guns and

crunch of falling bombs. I imagined this was the real commencement of hostilities against the British Isles. After a few moments I again came up; I wanted to stay in the flat all the time, but for the sake of my parents I went down. Davis tried to keep me down, but my answer to him, if he tries again, is that I am eighteen years of age, old enough for military service and to fight and die for my country. Fellows only a year my senior are up there shooting the raiders down, and within a year I to hope to be there. That is good enough for him. I popped indoors and finished off my dinner, and went once again to the top floor, but the smoke had cleared, and nothing was to be seen. Evidently not a great deal of really substantial damage had been done. The 'all clear' sounded soon after, and we went back to cold chicken. Damn, the only time for months we have had a chicken and then the Nazis have to spoil it.

23 August

I was awakened in the early hours of the 23rd by the pom-pom-pom-pom of anti-aircraft fire. I lay as if in a far-off existence, snuggling down in my bed; half-consciously I remember thinking 'I suppose the sirens will go soon' and they did within the next minute. Instantly my drowsy brain cleared, and I recalled with clarity that it was the 23rd, and *my* prophesied date for invasion seemed quite plausible. The moon was magnificent, silvery and shimmering, and looking about me I saw the dark, sharp contrast of the houses of London. As the sirens rose and fell, I thought how queer, how unreal, how like a vivid novel portraying in wild, fantastic form events to come it all was. And as I watched the houses drain themselves of people, like water going down a sink, and as the dull, vibrating noise of 'planes became audible in the distance I knew it was real. In this perspective I saw how cheap, how frail our life is. Just a puff, and a life, perhaps a great man or an ordinary person who liked his pint of beer and his pipe, was snuffed out, for ever, just like that. And I wondered exceedingly about that 'ever.' The gunfire had ceased now, and it was cold outside, so I went down into the warm, sticky atmosphere of the shelter. It was one constant hub of noise, of old women and squeaking babies, and men in their ridiculously long, overstriped pyjamas. Somehow I fitted myself in but only for a few minutes. I was back again with Dad indoors making tea when the 'all clear' went about 4 am.

Wednesday, 28 August (night)

I cannot say how tired I am. I have never known how much sleep means. Since the early hours of Friday morning the Nazi bombers have been over continuously, in consequence we have had warning after warning. It is now 9.45 pm—the warning went at 9 sharp. I will indulge in a brief resumé of the whole raid.

During the first few warnings on Friday and Saturday everyone was alert, prepared. Prepared for intensive bombing raids. We took cover. I only did so when circumstances forced me—i.e. in the office where it is compulsory to evacuate to the basement. At home, however, I always went to the top floor to view the south. But during the last few nights single German raiders have been systematically crossing the Metropolitan area. These lone raiders have occasionally dropped bombs, deliberately on the suburban districts, with the result that now every time a raider is reported the sirens have to be sounded. It is obvious that these raiders are only sent to affect our nerves, and try to shake our morale. They are termed in the Press as 'nuisance' raiders, and indeed that is the most fitting title for them. It is these that are responsible for keeping all Londoners awake and in their shelters for hours every night.

I am wondering, not anxiously, just how we intend counteracting these 'nuisance' raiders, for sleep is imperative and it looks as though we are to have another sleepless night. I am (another German—two came over then and I can still hear their drone dying over London) dark-eyed, have a terrible head, and long for Hell's own blizzard which would keep these damn infernal droning machines away for a night.

Monday, 2 September

There is nothing glamorous about this war. It is not a war. It's a mass butchery. In the olden days the civilian population was far removed from the scene of battle, they were respected by both sides. Now the Germans think fit to rain down their loads of death on harmless, defenceless civilians. Thank God Churchill is firm enough to refrain from ordering a retaliation bombing upon the German civilians. I fear I shouldn't be.

I suppose one day the sirens will cease to wail—but I cannot imagine it. It was wonderful coming home in the tube tonight during the raid and reading the *Standard*'s most uplifting leader. 'London' it was enti-tled. I looked at the people around me as I read it— yes, they would uphold, with their smiling faces, the future of mankind.

Week-end: 7–8 September

This is the most momentous week-end. Yesterday I lived my most momentous day—so far.

I set out on my old bike yesterday afternoon and pedalled through Carshalton, Burgh Heath, and on to Collie Hill—that great viewpoint overlooking all Sur-rey and Sussex to the South Coast.

I managed to secure a grandstand post on the small footbridge over the main road, and from here I ob-served for half-an-hour the antics of our fighters—but there were no Jerries. I tired of this, and mounting my bike cycled along the deserted roads, past the Home Guards and their barriers, and along the country lane in the direction of Chipstead. All along this lovely lane, alive with the beauty of summer, every field seemed to have its squadron of British fighters high above it. I have never seen so many planes. The sky was full of these 'Birds of Freedom.' Here and there people on foot, in cars, on bikes, had deposited themselves under the screen of trees, away from the eyes of Messer-schmitts. One and all remember the Nazis' machine-gunning zest. I continued, binoculars at the ready. An hour after the warning found me at the top of Chipstead Hill, lying full length in the thick grass, bin-oculars glued to my eyes, watching the many planes, and their landing on and off at a field some miles away.

Suddenly I thought to make Croydon, and remembered a marvellous viewpoint overlooking the 'drome from a hilltop some miles distant. I got every ounce of speed from the old bike, and simply flew down Chipstead Hill. I kept skidding to a standstill every so often and I picked out fresh tangles of aircraft, but they were always British. I had just passed the bottom of the deep valley between Chipstead and Woodmansterne when from a hole in the ground an air-raid warden told me to take cover. I conveniently ignored him, and bent hard on my pedals to climb the very steep hill. I was no more than half way up, and already overlooking the whole of the district south of Croydon, when masses of planes roared above me. British I thought, and concentrated on climbing the hill—one solitary figure on an expanse of road. Suddenly to my astonished ears the thud, the crunch of bombs came ever nearer. I looked out over the country—but pressed more eagerly to get to the top of the hill, from where I knew a better view was obtainable. I had no chance though to progress more than three-quarters of the distance. Pandemonium broke loose right above me. I jumped off my bike and looked up. It was the most amazing, impressive, riveting sight. Directly above me were literally hundreds of planes, Germans! The sky was full of them. Bombers hemmed in with fighters, like bees around their queen, like destroyers round the battleship, so came Jerry. My ears were deafened by bombs, machine-gun fire, the colossal inferno of machine after machine zooming in the blue sky. As I watched, spellbound, too impressed to use my glasses, a voice bellowed out 'Take Cover' and I realized then that it was the only sane thing to do. I jumped under a large and spreading oak, but no

sooner was I under its protecting leaves than I realized
the ridiculousness of my cover, and anyhow I could
not control my burning desire to see what was going
on, and as the noise became yet more intense I rushed
out—twisting, twirling, spinning, zooming, the universe was alive with lean, silver shapes. It came home
to me that in all probability it was the greatest massed
raid the country had ever known, and I guessed they
would be after Croydon. I remembered my viewpoint
for the airport was only another mile away, so under
that cloud of death I cycled furiously—but had got no
more than into the village of Woodmansterne when I
was compelled to dismount. Looking up—squadron
after squadron of Spitfires and Hurricanes tore out of
the blue, one by one they tore the Nazi formations into
shreds. 'Planes scattered left and right, and the terrible
battle came lower. As I stood on the neat grass verge of
the row of suburban houses, transfixed, I saw one
fighter (I very much fear ours) rush earthwards. With
ever increasing speed it fell, silently, to its last resting
ground, amongst the green of Surrey. I had no time to
dwell upon the fate of that man—I could not look
up—I just stood, and machine after machine rushed
frantically, screaming, it seemed, at me. I had no cover,
I held my glasses; I don't know what I felt, but I was
proving my theory—that in danger one knows no fear,
only a supreme feeling, indescribable. I would not dis-
own those minutes for Life itself.

9 September: 3.30 pm

THE CITY OF LONDON

I look out of my window, down on Lothbury, across
to the Bank of England. I see the beginning of Moor-

gate, Princes Street, and Gresham Street and Old
Jewry. I look up into the sky—dull, cloudy, grey; I listen; the noise which is echoing in my ears is of a
strange origin; it is banging and hammering, tinkling
and squeaking. Lorries pass under my window laden
with timber, cars stream by into Moorgate, great vans
and powerful motor-cycles. Buses grate their gears,
cars vomit huge clouds of exhaust. People surge
through the streets, hurrying, dragging great parcels,
gas-masks strapped round their bodies; this is London
today—a London industrious, dutiful, a City of calm,
of confidence, a City licking its hideous wounds in the
lull of the storm, a storm of machines which fly
through the air with the buzz of the bee, the sting of
the wasp. They come by night, they come by day. They
rain death upon the citizens of this, the greatest, most
learned, foremost City of the World, the Civilized
World!

How great an irony that strikes. Civilized indeed.
Nightly London buries its head into the ground, turns
out its lights, and sticks out its claws. Its long, tapering,
fingers of light prick the universe, probe the darkness.
They search for the birds of prey, the hawks of massacre who frequent our skies these September nights. The
bark, the spit of her lungs echo across the starlit heav-
ens and, turning yellow, orange, they flicker and dance
and pierce the armour of those birds. And as the morning comes, as the people set forth into the light of another day, they survey the sting of the hawks, weigh up
the damage showered upon their great, free City, note
with hardened brow the bloody mess which once was
their fellow man; this, these thoughts and sights are
stored, locked away in their deepest cell, until, one day,

in God's good time, they may without mercy exact from the nests of the prowlers of the night full and lasting revenge and fulfil that old and wisened proverb: 'An eye for an eye, a tooth for a tooth, a life for a life.'

So life goes on. As the clatter, the pounding of the labourer's tool becomes more incessant, I take leave of my meditation, I return once more into that which is London, Freedom, and I sigh, and breathe in the smoke, the smell of petrol fumes; I look at St Paul's and the figure of Justice, and I see myself looking back upon these long, dark, unreal days, when all the world seems mad, and lustful and sinful. I look back from a garden green, the sweet fragrance of red roses, roses of a New England, and I hear different noises—the sound of children playing, so gay and happy, and the yap of a spaniel and the meow of a kitten, and as I sit there, so content, so utterly happy, I find I hold the hand of a woman, a very beautiful, good and keen woman, and I see the son of my blood, and hers, set forth upon a clean, straight trail, and he, righteous, shall make his mark upon the world until he is acclaimed by mankind as the advocator of a free and noble world, in which all mankind lives and works in peace.

But I have memories . . .

10 September Later:

THE HEART OF A GREAT NATION

It is 1.10 pm on Tuesday, 10 September, 1940. I am sitting in my office on the second floor of the Royal Bank of Canada building in Lothbury. An air-raid siren sounded ten minutes ago. As I write under a grey sky, under a pall of 'acidy' smoke, within a few seconds' walk of wrecked and burning buildings, I take heart from the news I am to record.

I left the office this lunch hour at 12 precisely. I walked to the corner of King Street and Cheapside. My ABC was closed. Cheapside was a mass of charred debris; of firemen on ladders, hoses pouring jets of water into the charred and burning remains of elegant buildings of yesterday. Fire units, engines, troops in steel helmets move in the dense, choking clouds of smoke. Until the police move me along I stay and watch. The smoke rose high above St Paul's, obliterated the dome for minutes on end. Cheapside, in the heart of London, was stabbed. I moved along . . .

I saw a crowd, milling, cheering, near the Mansion House Station. More people rushed to the spot . . . I tore headfirst. What a crowd. Throbbing with anticipation, I fought my way through, jumped a police barrier, and heading off the crowd found the core of the excitement. Winston Churchill! I cheered, I yelled. I fought harder, and finally established myself in between Winston and his escort of the Commissioner of Police and an Officer of the Army. The crowd pressed on either side, but whether they mistook me for one of the party or not I cannot say; the fact remains I kept next to Churchill the whole route from the Mansion House Station to the Bank. I had my photograph taken countless times, and once had my hand on Churchill's coat. He looked invincible, which he is. Tough, bulldogged, piercing. His hair was wispy, wiry, tinted gingery. As he made his way through the smoke, through the City workers all crying 'Good old Winston'—'Give 'em socks'—'Good Luck'—and the culminating cry of 'Are we downhearted?' to the heaven-rising response to 'Nooooooo' which echoed round the City, round the world indeed, and warmed the 'cockles of our British hearts' and of all the free men in the world. It was magnificent, tremulous, stirring, dramatic. Amongst the 'ashes of London' stepped the man, his people, acclaimed, assured, and fulfilling the declaration that we will fight in the streets, in the fields, on the seas, in the air—that we would rather see London in ashes, but free and ours, than standing under the will of Hitler.

Churchill bought a flag outside the broken-windowed Mansion House, and I squeezed myself into the 'photo. He mounted the Mansion House steps and shook hands, presumably with the Lord Mayor; the people stood cheering themselves hoarse below, and we all stuck our thumbs up and yelled louder than ever for the Press photographers—and I guess I am in every one of their pictures. Next, Winston crossed to the bomb crater outside the Bank of England, and threw his cigar down upon the notice 'No Smoking—Danger Escaping Gas.' I could easily have retrieved the butt, but I had no desire to acquire such a souvenir—the sight, the memory is sufficient, and, I hope, the pictures. Winston stood on the bomb crater, waved, took off his bowlerish hat (how typical of the Churchill of the Sidney Street siege), sported his walking-stick, dug his left hand deep in his overcoat pocket. Approaching once again the crowds a young boy dashed up with an autograph album— Churchill signed. As he did so I had my hand on his sleeve, indeed I could not help myself, the crowd's pressure and enthusiasm was so terrific. Into his car and away—my hat, I certainly do seem to wangle my way into things—right by his side throughout his tour, the

records of which will find space in every future book of
history.

Tuesday, 24 September

Dad and I are on our own this week, Mother and
Alan being in St Alban's. I am more or less in the same
position as over a year ago when my people went to
Cornwall and I kept house for ten days. Yes siree, I am
the housekeeper. What fun!

Arriving home last night I set to work and made my
tea, then swept up the rooms, tidied all up, washed up
the crocks, tidied dirty corners. The sirens went at
about 7.50 signifying the nightly air-raid. But I stayed
in as I always do and got on with the housework. I
cleaned out Joey, our canary, and fed the goldfish. I
washed handkerchiefs and pyjamas and my favourite
white shirt. As I washed these articles guns were howl-
ing all around me, and just as I had put the kettle on
for my cocoa three bombs screamed down, shook the
building which swayed distinctly, and blew up. German bombers roared overhead, searchlights lit the sky.
Oh boy—I wonder what Lebkicher or even Kate would
have said if they could have seen me—in my dirty old
flannels, rolled-up blue open-neck shirt, hair ruffled,
and washing clothes amongst those eggs of whistling
death. I hung the clothes to dry in the bathroom, and
as it is not blacked out I had to grope my way to hang
the clothes, and my path was lit by constant gun
flashes, flaming onions and bursting shells. Phew. But
I must say I did enjoy myself, and I am extremely fond
of housework, and if ever I get married, then my wife'll
have to work like a Trojan and clean every nook and

cranny in the place, for I cannot bear untidiness. Anyhow the German bombers did great damage last night, and over seven bombs were dropped in our immediate vicinity, and I hear Wandsworth Common Station has been hit and busted up.

This morning I have washed up, cooked breakfast—eggs and fried bread—washed up, washed kitchen floor, and bathroom, made beds, tidied up in general, washed walls in bathroom and again put things in ship-shape order. Ironed (I love ironing) handkerchiefs.

25 September

Last night and in the early hours of this morning we experienced our worst aerial bombardment. We anticipated this in view of the RAF's extensive four-hour raid on Berlin the other day.

The alarm was given early, and until 10.30 we had a great deal of gunfire and bombs, in which period some fell exceedingly close. After 10.30 we had a comparative quiet period and Dad and I retired to bed. I was awakened by Dad calling at me to go in the hall at a quarter-to-one this morning. Above, an enormous number of enemy planes were roaring; our guns spoke I don't know how many times to the second. Great powerful guns just near us. Suddenly there came a whistle, shrill, followed by another nearer, yet a third, this time seemingly on top of us. Bombs! As they thudded down whistling, and then sudden silence, another salvo descended, and the fourth fell the other side of our flat, so did a fifth and sixth. In other words a stick of bombs had straddled our building. Well, we got back into bed, and without exaggeration it was un-doubtedly our busiest night. I was awakened almost hourly, and lay listening to the roar of jockeying planes, the scream of bombs, and the terrific noise of our guns which vibrated in my ears. I looked out—fires, searchlights, shells—a pandemonium.

Looking back this morning I am elated. Yes, elated. Last night Wandsworth had its very worst raid. History will prove that the area in which we live was the most frequently bombed of all London, including the East End. Every other area at least has its off and on nights, but we—well, every night is an on. (I write this during a raid. The alert was given ten minutes ago, but now the whistles telling of the immediate presence of hostile aircraft have warned all London to take cover. But my journal comes first. London doesn't all take cover—and I am not in the least degree perturbed, merely curious, indifferent.)

9 October

What is the prospect of Youth to-day? Upon the distant horizon there is no break in the war clouds, no dawn of respite from death. Youth can only see wars and sorrow, destruction and annihilation. Their ideals they see already cast down, trampled upon. There is no incentive to urge them to study for the higher extremes. Guns, bombs, planes are imprinted in our minds.

Myself, 18: I am able to see all the tangles and perplexities. I know that my whole life will be altered utterly, that my dreams of youth will not materialize as I had planned. I no longer see my path with my company, progressive, ambitious, but I see a void to which I drift the nearer. I know that soon I shall be in the fighting services, and am glad. But my worry is that perhaps my people will have to remain in the battle of London, and I feel confused, and cannot concentrate. It is one thing to go to war, and another to have the war come to you and yours.

Monday, 14 October

I look around me as I write: at the beer bottles, the match boxes, the newspapers and pictures, the radio, goldfish and canary—they are all symbols so secure which make bombing seem so utterly fantastic. Yet a German bomber roared overhead and I knew at any instant death and rubble may mark this spot. I hate to see canaries and goldfish; it brings home to me the futility of their lives, so completely devoid of anything but isolation. They cannot attain any end. It would drive me mad.

Near midnight there was an enormous red glow; it lit the whole of London. It was ten times brighter than the brightest summer's day. Then a series of explosions, more and still more, and the redness made us wonder. It was the new bomb I spoke of yesterday. A basket full of splitting death. Very near too. London is grotesque, insane. I cannot describe it—it's all too enveloping. Yet I live here in this city of death, of shocking reality and see my people's homes and persons killed and razed to the ground. I know any moment my turn may come. Yet, paradoxically, I know it won't. I know that despite the blood, the death, the absurdity of this life I shall survive. And I feel not one atom of fear or perturbance as I contemplate my future. Last night I slept as usual.

HELL

Sunday night, the 13th, saw one of the heaviest raids of the war upon South London. Balham, the suburb of ordinary people, was again bombed. One bomb has fallen in the centre of the High Road (obviously aimed for the railway close by) and I do not know whether the bus which I saw sunk in the crater this morning drove into it or whether it was blown there. Whatever, only a few inches of the double-decker is peeping above the roadway.

This bomb I think penetrated to the steel-encased Tube below the ground, and I hear too that something, by a million to one chance, went down the ventilator shaft of the Underground Station. The water main was burst and the flood rolled down the tunnels, right up and down the line, and the thousands of refugees were plunged into darkness, water. They stood, trapped, struggling, panicking in the rising black invisible waters. They had gone to the tubes for safety, instead they found worse than bombs, they found the unknown, terror. Women and children, small babes in arms, locked beneath the ground. I can only visualize their feelings, I can only write how it has been told to me, but it must have been Hell. On top of this there came a cloud of gas. People not killed outright were suffocated, the rest drowned, drowned like rats in a cage.

GOD

I have only heard this from a friend, and I can therefore only say that I believe it to be true.

A boy went to bed during the nightly raid. He awoke suddenly in the middle of the night to find no walls surrounded him, no staircase by which he could walk downstairs. Instead his bed was open to the four winds, resting on a floor held together only by girders. A bomb had struck his home and opened it completely, yet he lay in his bed, unharmed.

16 October

To-day I stand on the crossroads of my life. I can remain as I am, secure as these days will allow, or go forth into the unknown, ahead into the course of my life.

Amidst this City, wrecked by air-raids, I have to choose my destiny. My roads are varied, wide and narrow; one is bumpy, stoney, the other broad and smooth. At the end of one of them lies peace and happiness, supreme content, the other leads to an awful abyss; I can not see whether it be life or death. But I am done with the smooth. I want the uncertain, because without struggle I shall never be content. But here I will summarize the choice of my roads.

I can stay at this desk, with my firm when they move. Can enjoy luxury, change and new faces. I can walk in the Oxfordshire countryside for the office is moving away from this City. I can leave all the bombs and the guns, the 'planes and all this death and destruction. My bank book, too, can swell with ease and my aim of wealth be achieved. And after a while I can see my way to money, security and a foreign land. But I hate the thought of leaving my City in her hour of peril and need. I have lived in her so long, been bored with her ways, that if I should go when at last she has changed I feel that I should be running away. And, therefore, I shall not quit.

Yet I cannot stay so very long for despite it all I've had my fill, and conquered all and every fear, and I have once more become impatient with all this routine. The Merchant Navy is a very tough job, but one I cannot hope to see as much different from home; for these nightly bombs offer nothing worse than a torpedo out in the middle of sea. By doing so I can fulfil my ambition, of travelling around this world, in insecurity, by dint of slogging, roughing it, that is the trail I cleave.

But I do want to feel the speed of an aeroplane. I want to fly, and shoot the Nazi eagles. I want to be a pilot in the RAF.

Yet I must make a name for myself if I do want to write a book and write of all my childhood, of high ambitions, frustrated hopes, and all my enigma of thought. I want to lead this very world unto a better way of life, and point out all our futile ways and make a name for the very brave.

18 October

I SWEAR

Churchill promised us 'blood, sweat and toil'—how true he was. I have already sampled sweat and toil. Last night I sampled blood.

Just gone 8 last evening, Dad, Miller, Judd and myself were sitting in the dining room, comfortable in front of a roaring fire. I had just finished sweeping out the rooms and washing up my dinner things, and was just about to settle myself in *The Distant Drum,* a novel. Dad and the others were debating a Holmbury Court Register, to be filled in nightly showing which tenants were down in the shelter and who remained in their flats. This was to be handed to G.65 at midnight, thus in event of a bomb the rescue parties would know where to commence digging. As this procedure was going on a German bomber growled overhead. Off-handishly I listened, subconsciously, as one always does. I started to read my novel. He, that Jerry, had gone, I thought. Suddenly there was a roar like an express train, a hurtling, a tearing, all-powerful, over-whelming rush. Together we sprang to our feet. We got no further. The earth seemed to split into a thousand fragments. A wrenching jar I thought signified the splitting of our outside wall. The subsiding rush of materials took, it seemed, all off the back. We reached the hall. We all thought the bomb had fallen just a few yards outside the back, in Scotia's scrapyard. I quickly but calmly donned my suitcoat, put my keys in my pocket and my wallet in my inside pocket. I did this groping in the dark for I saw at a glance our blackout was not more. Strangely I found myself contemplating all this with a very aloof mind, almost of indifference, and I quietly smiled to myself; I was very unimpressed and for all the world it appeared to me as though this bomb was a normal occurrence. Ninety-nine people out of a hundred would, and did, complain of a turning of the stomach; not so me. Yet I knew then that death had nearly come to us. Outside there was a sti-fling, forbidding atmosphere. I stumbled over two masses of debris, clattered over piles of glass. The moon shone wanly upon this uncanny nightmare.

Women in the hall were dizzy. I rushed outside in the front. I saw at once all the windows of the flats had been blasted open or out. This I pointed out to Dad and Miller who together went down to the shelter, which since the explosion had rapidly filled, and told all the tenants to be extremely careful when they went into their flats in view of the torn down blackout. I meanwhile pelted headlong under a barrage of bursting shells along the Upper Tooting Road, past shopkeepers resignedly clearing up their smashed shop fronts, up Beechcroft and so into Fishponds Road, which as the crow flies lies not fifty yards at the back of us. It was a turmoil of rushing, calm, tin-hatted wardens. Two demolition squads and rescue parties roared up. I counted ten ambulances. I quickly entered into the centre of the crowd, a crowd only of nurses, wardens, firemen. And there, amidst the dark suburban street, standing on charred debris of every description, I found a new Perry. I confronted war in its most brutal savagery, I beheld blood, wounded, dying. I stood transfixed. My stomach did not turn, but from afar, yet so intimately, I found my brain dully registering sights of gore; I found I stood by the side of a little boy, his head a cake of blood, his arms—I knew not where they were. A small, plump, efficient voluntary nurse put her arms round him. He cried, every so often, very sobbingly for his Mummy. His Mummy was not to be seen. Quietly the nurse fingered his wounds—in a concise, firm, business-like voice, as if she was talking to a Mothers' meeting, 'Take him away immediately. Hospital case,' and turned her attention to the next. That nurse was in complete charge, she swayed her audience. The little boy, head wrapped in towels, was gently laid upon a stretcher, passed softly along inside the waiting ambulance, still sobbing, though fainter, for his dear Mummy. I turned from that pathetic, heart-rending scene. I was oblivious of the falling shrapnel, of the clamouring guns, of the German bombers still roaring overhead. I heard from afar the wardens tell me to get under cover, for I was the only one without a steel helmet. Yet somehow that seemed very silly and petty to me then. I moved under the shielded light of a warden's torch; so shielded for we knew instinctively that the bombers might at any moment rain fresh death upon us. I saw through the waning moon the wrecked dwelling-houses, saw a warden rush headlong up the stairs of one of the doomed houses. I moved nearer to death—sitting on a chair, sobbing, convulsing, making distant moans, was a stout old lady; I judged that by her red and yellow spotted dress. By her side stood a quiet and silent girl, holding her arm, as if the contact would assure this wounded, bloody carcase that she was in the hands of God. Her face I could not see. It was covered with a huge piece of cloth, slitted for the nose to breathe. Underneath seeped streams of blood, and as I watched the blood clotted itself into little mounds. I shut my eyes tight for one instant. I wanted to shriek defiance at those bombers prowling even now above our heads. Then, as suddenly, this passion left me. I felt weak, impotent at the sight. My mind flashed back—if only—but I knew no first-aid, and I had never before so much wanted to be a doctor. The wardens formed a protective barrier around this slowly heaving woman, and under the light of a torch I saw her legs, cut and bleeding. A two-inch-long red mark signified where a

piece of metal had embedded itself into her leg. They
lifted her skirts—I did not look. I walked across to a
young, it seemed, and slim woman. She was sitting so
patiently on a chair, drinking water. I saw only the
back of her head—it was enough. Blood, blood, blood,
it oozed from her scalp, formed cakes on her skin. Oh
God . . . I breathed a soft prayer. All this while I had
bit hard upon my pen which I had been holding in my
hand, and after I had put it into my pocket I could not
find it, and next to those wounded, smashed bodies
I felt in all my pockets and in my wallet. I found my
pen . . . I wondered how I could trouble about such a
trifle when around me lives were being fought for. I
turned, I spoke to Mr Humphreys the post warden of
G.65, now in supreme command. He asked me to
stand by ready to take a message after I had volunteered my service. I was amazed at his efficiency: I ad-
mire the man. Some minutes later I ran back along the
soft moonlit road, soft due to the mist which hung on
the evening, as if a cloak to hide this wounded City. I
went up to the flat, and surveyed the damage. But
firstly I stood and said a prayer, to ask God to relieve
their suffering and to give us strength to fight this war.
I then looked at the photograph of Binnie, then at my
own—it dawned upon me that death had struck just
fifty yards away, in a straight line with our flat, the
other side of Scotia's—that's how near. War had come
to Tooting, to Holmbury Court, to me. War? nay murder, worse. Just a second later or a second earlier and
that bomb would have struck at me, and I saw those
blood-caked people . . . I thanked God, and wondered
if I had deserved to have been spared. After all, was I
so good and righteous as those people across the way?

They were an ordinary family, probably never been out of London in their lives; they had been no doubt just happily, as present conditions would allow, eating their supper, thinking the war very remote from them—and then, their lives were cut, they were victims of Hitler's massacre. I SWEAR that I'll revenge them, I swear I will! I will not be a member of a bomber crew—never! If I thought for one moment I was a cog in bringing about such terrible tragedy I would rather be shot. My job is clear. I will be a fighter pilot, and I will shoot mercilessly the bloody Hun from out of the skies. I will fire callously at their bombers' crews, I will know no pity. I will blast these murderers, assassins, devils of all that is evil from out of the skies. May God grant me strength. For I have experienced the horror of war, the blood which has to be paid. If they had been soldiers—different. But women, children, my breed—I will not rest until I have fulfilled my vow.

"THE TROUBLES"

IN

NORTHERN IRELAND

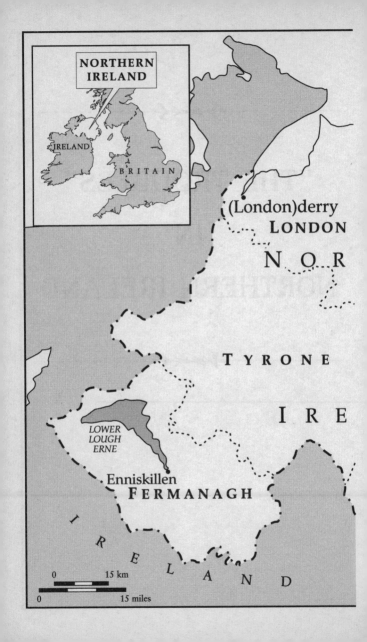

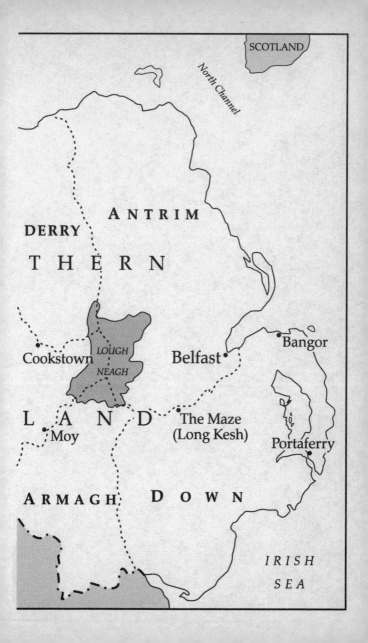

Introduction

I n 1969 animosities between Catholics and Protestants in Northern Ireland escalated into what is called "the Troubles," three decades of violence during which more than thirty-four thousand shootings and fourteen thousand bombings resulted in the wounding of over forty thousand people and the loss of more than thirty-one hundred lives.

Eyewitness to this widespread violence, the generation that is known in Northern Ireland as "children of the Troubles" has never known a permanent peace. In these true stories, memoirs, essays, diaries, letters, and a poem, nine of them tell what it has been like to grow up in a painfully divided country and what it means to them that, after decades of murder and destruction, there is now a possibility of a lasting peace.

Many of us who have not grown up in Northern Ireland have difficulty understanding what would bring members of two Christian communities to fight to the death with one another. In fact, the Catholic/Protestant conflict is more of an ethnic conflict between two culturally distinct groups over land and civil rights than a war about religious doctrine.

One clear indicator that the violence stems from an ethnic conflict rather than a religious one is that it predates the Protestant Reformation by several centuries.

In fact, ethnic violence has been the rule rather than the exception for over eight hundred years in Northern Ireland. Still, some of the major roots of the current Troubles can be found in the seventeenth century, when the British government sent thousands of Scottish Protestants (many of them Presbyterians) to confiscate land owned almost entirely by Catholics. By 1703 the Scottish settlers, backed up by British military force, had taken 95 percent of the land in the six counties that make up Northern Ireland today.

Not only did the Scottish Protestant settlers take the land from the Irish Catholics, who had barely managed to scrape a living from it as it was, but when many of the Protestants were successful in the new country because of the wealth they had brought and the support of the British government, they were not inclined to share the bounty with the Irish Catholics, whom they regarded as a somewhat primitive and barbaric people.

Massacres and rebellions defined the next two centuries in Ireland. All in all, the Protestants killed more Catholics than Catholics killed Protestants, and the northeast corner of the country became a Protestant stronghold while most of the Catholics who had lived there migrated to the south and west of Ireland. This mass displacement of the majority of the people who had inhabited Northern Ireland was in many respects more consequential than the loss of lives that occurred on both sides. Events connected with this displacement are firmly etched in the ethnic memory of both communities, and annual commemorations of these events reinforce and maintain the centuries-old sectarianism that characterizes Northern Ireland today.

Great Britain was seen by the Catholics as the real enemy behind the persecution they had received at the hands of the Scottish Protestants. Even many descendants of the Scottish planters were none too fond of England's control of them and their land. Protestants were, in fact, some of the major leaders of the home rule movement that culminated in the Easter Rising, an armed rebellion of Irish patriots against British troops on Easter Monday of 1916 in Dublin.

Great Britain's execution of these Irish patriots sharply increased Catholic demands for home rule and eventually led to a war for independence. At the conclusion of that war, in 1921, Britain relinquished its hold on the southern twenty-six counties of Ireland that had a strong Catholic majority while firmly retaining control of the Protestant-dominated, northeast six counties that are known as Northern Ireland today.

If the populations of what had become two separate countries in 1922—now known as the Republic of Ireland and Northern Ireland—had been exclusively of one religion or the other, perhaps the peoples of Ireland could have peacefully coexisted on the same island. But a sizable Catholic minority remained in Northern Ireland when Ireland was divided, and the division of the country did nothing to decrease the sectarian strife there.

Gerrymandering and oppressive voting regulations in Northern Ireland gave the Protestants nearly complete control of local and national government, including the police force of the country, the Royal Ulster Constabulary. Public housing was unfairly allocated, and Protestants were encouraged to hire only Protestants so that many more Catholics than Protestants were forced into poverty in the years following the division of Ireland.

With the relative prosperity that followed World War II came changes in social policies in Northern Ireland. Free education—albeit nearly completely segregated education—was extended to Catholics as well as Protestants, and Catholics began to hope for a better future for their children. Still, there remained widespread inequities in employment, housing, and the administration of civil rights. Many Catholics in Northern Ireland believed that the only way to redress these ills would be to join the Republic of Ireland—with its 95 percent Catholic majority—and become one nation again, free of British rule. Obviously, this prospect had little appeal for Protestants, who would become the minority in a united Ireland.*

On August 24, 1968, the history of Northern Ireland changed forever when, inspired in part by Dr. Martin Luther King, Jr., and also by Vietnam War protests and the 1968 Paris student revolt, four thousand nonsectarian civil rights activists, who were perceived by Protestant Unionists as Catholic Nationalists, took to the streets in what they intended to be a peaceful protest against discrimination and injustice. They marched again on October 5 in the city of Londonderry (Derry) and were attacked by the Protestant-dominated Royal Ulster Constabulary.

Another march, similarly intended to be nonsectarian, was held in January of 1969. Caught on film and broadcast round the world, police and civilian attacks

---

*Demographic experts estimate that if current population trends continue, Protestants could become a minority in Northern Ireland by the year 2015 and perhaps even sooner in certain areas of the country.

on peaceful civil rights marchers set the stage for the decades of murder and mutilation carried out by paramilitary organizations on both sides of the sectarian divide as well as by the police and the British military.

In 1969 bombings on both sides began in earnest, and Bernadette Devlin (a very outspoken twenty-one-year-old Catholic political activist) won a seat in Parliament, a wake-up call to the level of unrest in the Catholic community. In August of that year British troops arrived on the streets of Northern Ireland, and by September they had erected the Berlin Wall of Belfast, the first of many so-called Peace Lines, that confirmed the absolute division between the two communities and the fact that they could not live together in peace.

Most of the writers whose work appears in this book have known since they were toddlers that because they were born into either a Protestant or a Catholic family in Northern Ireland, they were destined to take sides and suffer the consequences. Yet many barely knew the "enemy." Northern Ireland is so divided that many young people do not even meet a member of the other religious community until they are in their teens.

From the moment children are born in Northern Ireland they begin to live in a majority Protestant or a majority Catholic neighborhood. They go to either a Catholic or a Protestant school, and their friends are likely to be exclusively one or the other. They are taught to shop only in their "own" shops in some towns and, eventually, to socialize only in their "own" pubs. And, of course, when they die they will go to a segregated graveyard. In Belfast even the taxis divide along religious lines. And in some parts of the country the sidewalks are painted to designate political/religious loyalties.

Children absorb differences in language and perspective that set them apart from one another for the rest of their lives. If you are Catholic, for example, you call Northern Ireland's second largest city "Derry"; if you are Protestant, it is "Londonderry." If you are Catholic, you call the nearly three decades of the Troubles a "war"; if you are Protestant, you are careful to point out that there has been a terrorist uprising, not a war, in Northern Ireland.

In fact, even the name you call your country will be in question. If you are raised in a Catholic family wanting the reunification of Ireland, you will refer to "the North of Ireland" as your homeland or call it "The Six Counties," rather than making it sound as if it were a separate country called Northern Ireland. And if you were raised in a Protestant environment, you will be more likely to call your country Northern Ireland or Ulster.

In addition to the difficulties of learning to live in such a segregated country, some Protestant and Catholic children are coerced into running secret errands for terrorists and assembling and hiding their weapons.

Although the majority of people in Northern Ireland abhor violence and take no part in it themselves, virtually every family in Northern Ireland has had members beaten, tortured, or murdered, and the country's children have been witness to it all. For this is not a private war, conducted behind closed doors, nor a war where the men go away to fight the enemy. This is an everyday, in-your-face war, where the enemy lives on the next block and speaks (nearly) the same language.

Prior to the recent paramilitary cease-fires, it was almost inconceivable that anyone would put his or her experiences of the Troubles into print. Reprisals could be swift and deadly, however small or unintended the provocation. The motto in Northern Ireland, taught by parents on both sides of the sectarian divide, has long been "Whatever you say, say nothing." Sadly, this has meant that a whole generation has been silenced about their fears, their anger, their losses—and that, with few exceptions, there is little in the literature of Northern Ireland to reflect the complex realities of living in a country of 1.6 million people torn apart by ethnic strife.

Now the women and men, girls and boys, in this book not only are courageous enough to tell their own stories of what has happened to them and their families during the Troubles, they also convey how much it means to them that there is, for the first time in their lifetimes, a hope of permanent peace in their country.

Some of the writers have chosen to use the tools of fiction in telling their stories, but all have assured me that their work is autobiographical and that the events they described really happened to them, although a few of the writers did, on occasion, change names and places to protect other people.

It is important that we listen to these writers and learn from their experience. Northern Ireland is certainly not the only violently divided country in the world, and the lessons these writers have to teach us are applicable in Bosnia, Israel/Palestine, South Africa, and

Rwanda, to name a few, as well as in every city in the United States where racial and ethnic strife causes us to live in fear of one another.

As you read about the tragedy in Northern Ireland, I hope you will be thinking of your own country, your own state, your own neighborhood, and how distinctions we have found it necessary to make between our fellow human beings and ourselves are contributing to the destruction of our human family. For this is not just about Northern Ireland, it is about us—all of us—who would try to live peaceably together on this planet, no matter how great our differences.

I have edited all work for consistency in spelling, grammar, and punctuation and occasionally decreased the length of prose pieces. I have retained the writers' own British/Irish spelling and syntax. Explanations contained in parentheses are the writers'. For authors under twenty-one years of age, I have specified the age at which their work was written at the beginning of their story or poem.

LAUREL HOLLIDAY
1996

John McConnell

*W*hen I asked thirty-five-year-old John McConnell what stands out in his life, he said, "the Troubles. I've always been nervous . . . never calm . . . and with the cease-fires I'm just the same." Even though there had been no shootings for over a year, John told me that he still jumped whenever he heard fireworks. "I've got it in my head," he said, 'Oh, that's shooting! That's shooting!' "

John was brought up in a conflict area near the Castle-reagh Road in East Belfast, where he says he knew that every weekend there was going to be trouble. "Whenever you saw a gang standing on the corner, you knew they were just waiting for the Army and the police to come up so they could start trouble." Sometimes the violence was so bad that his mother kept him and his four brothers in the house.

As his story shows, John was always open to friend-ships on the other side of the divide and, as it turned out, his early romantic relationships were with Catholic girls. That made him a target for both sides, but somehow he was able to carry on peacefully.

Several years ago John was targeted by the IRA partly because of a mistaken identity and partly because he cooks for the Army. Of this terrifying time he says: "The police asked me if I wanted to move house or if I wanted *to change my job. I said no. But I was putting things up against the doors. I thought someone was going to bust the doors down. The police asked if I wanted to arm myself. But I just wouldn't have a gun in the house."*

This was just a few months before the cease-fires, which, when they were announced by both sides, helped a little to put John's mind at ease. He concludes his story, in fact, with the statement that there is peace now in Northern Ireland, which was a bit optimistic perhaps, even considering that it was written during the cease-fires.

Today John is living happily with his partner and their children. He says, "So long as my kids are okay, I'm okay. I love my family. I live for my kids."

But one thing is missing for John. He misses Eamon, the childhood friend who is the subject of his story. He wrote this story in hopes that Eamon (whose last name is Marks) will read it and get in touch with him through the publisher of this book.

Eamon

This is my story of meeting Eamon in the times of the Northern Ireland Troubles.

I moved into an estate [housing project] on the outskirts of Belfast when I was about fifteen years old. I just hung about my house for the first few days. Then one day I was playing football by myself when two boys came up to me and asked me if I would like to play football with them. I said "yes," so we went over to a field where boys were picking teams.

One of the boys who asked me if I wanted to play

football with them was called Eamon. I realised he must be a Catholic as the boys were laughing and saying that Eamon's team was Celtic. This was the first time I had met a Catholic and he was just like the rest of us. And a good footballer too!

When we stopped playing Eamon said he would walk round with me as he lived not far from me—about five doors away.

The conversation was mostly about football until I asked him if he supported the Celtics [a Catholic team with a Catholic following from Northern Ireland]. "Yes," he said and then he told me that he was a Catholic. There was a silence for a while between us and then he said he would see me later.

So later that night he called for me and we did what we did most nights after that which was play more football and go to the school youth club.

I got to know Eamon better and he told me he'd lived on the estate for four years now and that he and his mother were the only Catholics in the estate. But he never talked about that much. He told me he was not interested in the Troubles. He only had time for his mother as his father had passed away.

Eamon was not what I thought Catholics were like—cross-eyed and dirty—although I had never met any of them up to now. Eamon was a tall, skinny lad—always well-dressed and with black straight combed hair. He was quiet and helpful.

One day he took me by surprise by saying he was going out to collect bonfire wood for the 11th July [eve of Orange Day, a Protestant holiday] and he wanted to know if I was going to help him. And I always thought that the Catholics went down to Dublin for the 11th–

12th July to get away! He did his bit for the bonfire. We must have collected four doors and a lot of old tyres. Here was a Catholic lad out collecting wood for the Protestant bonfire. Nowadays we would be lucky to see a Catholic near a bonfire, let alone helping collect for one!

I saw Eamon a lot more now, but not in the daytime as he went to a Catholic school. One day I asked him would he have liked to have gone to our school and he said he would have loved to go to our school but he had to go to his own school because of his Catholic "ways."

That night I called for him. It was raining heavy and his mother, Pauline, came out and asked me did I want to come in as Eamon was upstairs. This was the first time I was in Eamon's house. I sat down and I noticed a cross and a picture of the Virgin Mary up on the wall.

Eamon's mother asked me did I like living in the estate. I said yes. After that it was quiet because I did not know what to say to her. Then she offered me some lemonade and then Eamon came in and asked his mother could I go up to his room. She said yes, so we went up. Eamon's room was like mine—pop posters and football posters—only he had Celtic posters up! He told me about the time when there were only about five Catholic families living on the estate and one night he heard a lot of shouting and screaming. He looked out the back window of his house and saw a Catholic family moving out and a crowd around his own house. He said he panicked and ran downstairs and told his mother. She locked all the doors and drew the curtains. Then there was a knock at the door.

Eamon said his mother was screaming and they

heard a lot of screaming outside. He looked out the window and saw a group of women. They shouted to him to open the door and he said he opened it because he knew a lot of the women at his door. They came in and they asked where his mother was. She was in the kitchen and they got her to calm down as she was in hysterics.

I asked Eamon how did he feel and he said he felt scared and shaking. He felt like running out of the house and not stopping. But he also said he worried about his mother.

He told me that one of the women from the estate had told him that men from other areas had come into the estate to get all of the Catholic families out. The women said they would help keep Eamon and his mother safe from the men. The women stood outside their door and front window and shouted to these men to go away. He said it lasted about twenty minutes. But it was like all night to him.

Then the men went away but they shouted that they would be back. But this never happened.

His mother would not move house but she was still afraid to go out of the house for about six months and she had to get help from the doctor. Eamon told her he didn't want to move either. The women of the estate helped him and his mother a lot and this is why they stayed in the estate.

That night really told me what kind of person Eamon was—caring and helpful, and he loved his mother.

I got to know his mother well and so did my own mother. The 11th night came and we were celebrating. Eamon was with us and we were singing "The Sash" [a

Protestant anthem] and he joined in. He even sang the "Billy Boys," another well-known Protestant song!

It was not long after this that there were a lot of tit-for-tat shootings going on—Protestants shooting Catholics and Catholics shootings Protestants. The trouble was getting worse. Eamon still never said much about the Troubles that were going on. That was his nature.

After one night at the school youth club we walked home and said the usual things—"see you later," "see you tomorrow." But I never did. That night someone shot two shots through Eamon's window. I heard the bangs and went downstairs. My father told me to stay in the house, so I looked out of my brother's window and saw a crowd at Eamon's house. Then I saw an ambulance come and take someone away.

My mother came up and told me that Eamon was shot. But he was okay as he was shot in the lower leg. I felt numb. And I felt hatred for the ones who did this. Why Eamon, I just kept asking myself.

Next morning I saw a lorry moving all of the furniture out of Eamon's house. I ran downstairs and I asked one of the men where was Eamon and he just said he was in hospital and he was okay.

Later I found out it was one of his uncles moving house for him and his mother. I never heard of where he moved to, but there was a rumour going around that he moved to England and is living there now. I still think about him and wonder how he would feel now that there is peace in Northern Ireland.

Margaret McCrory

*M*argaret McCrory, now in her thirties, writes and raises her family on a farm seven miles out of Cookstown in County Tyrone. The crisp autumn afternoon that I went to visit her, we sat behind closed doors in front of a turf fire in her living room while her teenage daughters made a fancy tea in my honor and her young son played ball with his friends and his dog in the front yard. Occasionally one of the girls would come in to stoke the fire with another piece of peat, which is dug from the earth, dried in rectangular chunks, and used as fuel.

"You must think I'm a fool," Margaret began our conversation. What tumbled out in the half hour we talked privately is that Margaret herself sometimes wonders if she did the right thing in deciding to return to Northern Ireland to marry and raise a family after her own parents had emigrated from Northern Ireland to America when she was thirteen. Her teenage daughter, who visits her grandparents often, is certain that life in the States far outshines life on a farm, seven miles from anywhere, in the middle of Northern Ireland. She is never more certain of this than during lambing season, when she must take her turn staying up all night to await expected births, or when she goes to her job washing dishes at a Cookstown hotel after school—the only part-time job she could find.

Yet for Margaret the importance of the family living in

*a place they can truly call home outweighs all of the diffi-
culties—even those caused by the Troubles, to which
Cookstown is no stranger. After a year of the cease-fires,
while most towns were disassembling barricades and relaxing security, I saw soldiers patrolling with rifles aimed
and ready to fire near a barbed-wire-covered Cookstown
Royal Ulster Constabulary (police) station.*

*In the following story, Margaret conveys the absolute
terror of a child's being trapped in the crossfire in Belfast
during the conflagration that resulted from the institution
of internment. This policy, which was sanctioned by the
government of Great Britain in response to the violence in
Northern Ireland, allowed the police to imprison people
they deemed suspicious, without the necessity of charging
them with a crime or producing evidence.*

Internment

August 9, 1971, is a day I will remember as long as I
live. We were emigrating to America the next day but
that's not why I'll remember that date. That was the
night of Internment. I was only thirteen at the time,
but just thinking about that day still brings back the
knotted feelings in my stomach.

I was supposed to feel excited about leaving and
also sad to be saying good-bye to our friends and
neighbours. But we woke up that morning to a strange
silence outside. We found ourselves whispering to
each other and sneaking looks out the windows. There
was nothing out there at all—no people, no cars, not
even the dogs were barking. It was eerie.

We felt something big was about to happen, but when? The waiting was the worst feeling I've ever felt. I don't know if we would have sensed so much tension if my Mum hadn't kept repeating over and over again, "Please, Lord, get us out of here." She looked and acted like she was scared to death and I suppose some of that rubbed off on us. We were very subdued all day. The funny thing was there wasn't a bite in the house, yet no one complained they were hungry.

Late afternoon, and there was still no activity outside. By this time we were all nervous wrecks. We had nothing in the house to occupy us—just a couple of mattresses and our suitcases. Hugh, who was nine, was so nervous that he made himself sick. Mum made him lie down on the mattress in the boys' room on the second floor. Eileen, eleven, was walking around like a zombie, staring straight ahead with huge eyes. She was scary. David, eight, and Maria, seven, were playing quietly on the bare floor, which was really unusual for them. Mum and I took it in turns to peek out of the windows.

Mum had gone into the kitchen to brush [sweep] the floor when the shooting began. We could hear the bullets whizzing over the house and ricocheting off the corrugated iron on the factory wall behind our house. The bullets smashed through the kitchen window. Mum dropped the brush and ran. To this very day she still complains about leaving a pile of dirt on the floor.

Hugh was crying upstairs and Eileen was screaming her head off. Between the deafening noise inside and the explosive noises from outside, we felt like we were in the middle of World War III. All the shooting seemed to be at the back of the house where the boys' room was so we dragged Hugh and the mattress up to the third floor where our room overlooked the front of the house. We all huddled together on the mattresses.

It was very hot but when Mum opened the window a little bit we could feel our throats begin to burn. Which meant that there was tear gas out there, and from past experience we knew what that could do to you. Your throat would begin to burn and your eyes would sting like mad. Then you would feel violently sick. It was a horrible feeling so we quickly shut the window.

The Uzis were going mad out there—the noise was incredible!—and Eileen couldn't stop screaming. I was scared but I also felt excited and very curious. I really wanted to know what was going on out there so every chance I got I would sneak a look outside. I could see men with guns running up our street. They saw me and shooed me in by gesturing with their hands to get down. Mum made me sit with them on the mattresses, but Eileen's screaming was driving me mad so I finally told her that they weren't going to kill her because I was going to do it first. She quieted down to loud whimpering instead.

We could see the orange glow of petrol bombs exploding and hear the bang of plastic bullets being fired. The boys were good at recognizing the sounds because they used to collect spent cartridges after nights of violence. But this was the worst we had ever seen.

Finally Maria, David, and Hugh went to sleep. Mum had to comfort Eileen, who was scared out of her mind. There was too much going on to even think of sleep. Every so often there would be a slight lull and I would run to the window. The sky was really bright now. The barricades were burning so as to keep the soldiers out. I could see men outside shooting their guns up the avenue. They were hiding behind walls, bins, poles—anything at all. It was like watching television. When several bullets hit the wall outside our window Mum made me lie down again.

We heard people shouting for Father Murphy, our parish priest, to come and give someone the Last Rites. Ten minutes later we heard shouts of "They killed Father Murphy!" "They shot him!" "Three bodies on top of each other!" Mum and I could only look at each other in shock. Father Murphy was our friend. He taught Hugh and David how to box. He had been at our house only yesterday—they must be wrong.

They weren't. Ten men died that night, all from our street. Father Murphy had been shot dead while giving a man the Last Rites. And when another man went to help Father Murphy he had been killed as well.

It was very hard lying there listening to the *rat-a-tat* of the gunfire and not think that someone else might be dead. The excitement was gone and fear and deep sadness were left. We lay there until morning when, finally, all noises stopped and we could hear our neighbours outside.

They were clustered together exchanging war stories and talking about Father Murphy. We were next on their agenda. We were never going to get out, they said, and no one was going to risk his life to get us out. I think they were a bit jealous.

Mum didn't give up. She asked everybody until one man with an old post office van said yes.

We had an awful time getting through burnt-out barricades and around overturned lorries—sometimes even human barricades. After many detours we finally reached the airport to find no planes were flying that day. We were bundled into a minibus and driven to Dublin.

We were still in shock from the night before. Even after twenty-four hours with no food none of us complained that we were hungry. Every time we heard Father Murphy's name mentioned on the radio we cried our eyes out but Mum just kept repeating "Thank God we're out!" That's all she would say.

She was dead right though. Thank God we did get out.

Margaret E. Simpson

*W*hen I visited Margaret Simpson on an icy, blustery autumn day in Belfast, three generations were awaiting me: Margaret, her husband, her four-year-old daughter Amy, and Margaret's mother, who had obviously been baking all day in anticipation of the Devon tea the family would share with me.

Now in her thirties and living in a sedate neighborhood of detached homes on quiet streets with her husband and two young daughters, Margaret grew up in what she calls a "kitchen house" near the Shankill Road with two rooms up and two rooms down and the toilet in the backyard. She remembers that when street fighting with Catholics would erupt, neighbors would come into her family's house to collect whatever they could find for barricades. One day they took her mother's ironing board.

Margaret has been writing poetry since age seven. In 1994 she joined a writers' group and really began to take her writing seriously. She has had a number of her poems published in the group's magazine, Stadium.

The terrifying events that Margaret writes about in "Kneecapped" occurred when she was fifteen, but it wasn't until 1995 that she could bring herself to write about them.

Tragically, kneecapping is a frequent form of "policing" done by paramilitaries of all persuasions in Northern Ire-

land. Intended to reinforce their power in their own communities, to discourage any possible disclosures to the police or Army, and to frighten people into compliance, maiming a person in this way often means they will never walk or function normally again.

Kneecapped

He came to our door on a Wednesday night
As I was about to leave,
Walk my granny home, at least halfway
Up the back Shankill into Indian territory.
I suppose I thought myself brave at fifteen
To face Ardoyne alone,
Well, almost.
He rang the doorbell, normal enough,
Asked if he might use our phone,
An emergency of sorts, his voice faltered,
He slumped forward, and as though in slow motion
Fell in the hall at my feet.
My mother and her mother dragged him in,
Laid him on our sofa, my dad's leather sofa.
I watched as Granny at his feet,
Ripped his trouser from ankle to knee.
"Went in behind the knee out the foot,"
She said with calm authority.
I brought the basin in, just as I was told,
Crystal clear water turned crimson
When the towel from his leg was rung out.
The ambulance was on its way.
Two men appeared at our door almost from nowhere,
Strangers.

Checked he was getting attention
Then as they had come they vanished.
The police came, they noted his words,
Shot from a passing car.
The ambulance took him.
And we knew he lied.

P. J. Quinn

BELFAST

*W*hen the Troubles began, in 1969, P. J. Quinn was twenty years old and living as he still does in West Belfast, one of the most affected areas of the city. "Some of my neighbours were killed in gun and bomb attacks," he says, "and I saw several shootings at close range as well as discovering the body of a murder victim dumped in an alleyway."

In his story, P. J. captures the intense feelings of terror that could come over anyone in the Troubles, particularly a young man home alone while parents are away for a weekend.

Today P. J. is a librarian, and he is working on a screenplay. No stranger to publishing, he had an epic-length poem published in The Irish Review, *a prestigious literary journal, in 1989.*

Clutch of Fear

I can still recall those dark, fear-filled days of 1975. There were various theories about how and why the bitter and bloody feud between the Official and Provisional wings of the Republican movement [IRA] began but the one that I thought most reliable was that the seeds of it were sown during the summer when the Secretary of State for Northern Ireland started releasing internees [prisoners] who belonged to the Provisionals. This goodwill gesture, it was hoped, would be reciprocated by the Provo leadership in terms of a scaling-down of their terrorist campaign. If memory serves me right it made little difference to the bombing and killing except that in one respect—largely unforeseen even by senior intelligence experts—it made it worse:

When the Provo prisoners were returned to their communities they found that the Official (Marxist-oriented) IRA had taken advantage of their absence to increase their influence in Provo-controlled areas by muscling in on their lucrative empire of bars, night-clubs, illegal shebeens [alcohol outlets], one-armed bandit joints, and other places of entertainment. Naturally the Provos resented this and they held meetings to discuss what to do about it. The course of action they decided upon was characteristic of their thinking as a whole—they decided to exterminate the Officials and their sympathisers. And the emphasis should be placed on "sympathisers," for very few of the Provos' victims during this brutal vendetta could have been described as "activists." The Official IRA had been on permanent cease-fire since 1972 when their leaders renounced violence in favour of political action. Officials and their supporters organised themselves into "Republican Clubs" which concentrated on working-class nonsectarian politics. It was these Republican Club members, many of whom had never held a gun in their lives, who bore the brunt of the Provo purge. While the bloodletting was not confined to Belfast, it was most intense there.

I don't know what the first incident was that actually sparked the feud. Numerous stories, put about by both sides, circulated in the streets and in the newspapers. Consensus on such matters is always difficult, but the Republican feud, like most feuds, began in "little" things and quickly spiralled out of control. And I definitely do recall that, whoever struck the first blow, the merciless and cold-blooded nature of the murders chilled all decent people to the bone and brought real terror to thousands of homes throughout Northern Ireland.

Among the more ominous developments was the spraying of homes belonging to the Officials and their supporters with red "death crosses," allowing the Provo killer squads to identify their targets with ease. They bombed each other's bars and clubs; Provos hurled petrol bombs into Official business premises; Officials drove to Provo nightspots with rifles strapped to their motorcycles and raked everyone inside with gunfire; workers were forced to flee their jobs; families were intimidated out of their homes by means of threatening phone calls, black bereavement bows tied to gateposts, bullets dropped through letter boxes. Fear spread from one side of Belfast to the other. Doors were locked and bolted after dark and furniture was piled up against them to slow down killers who might try to sledgehammer their way in. The women of the Republican areas, whose sons, husbands, and brothers were the targets, came onto the streets in impromptu demonstrations, chanting, "End the feud, end the feud!" But more lives were to be lost before they got their wish.

I was alone when the doorbell rang in the early hours—my parents were away on autumn break [vacation]. I woke up instantly because my thoughts were choked with the horror of the latest feud killing the previous night. A Provo with a machine gun had shot his way into a house just a hundred yards from my own and opened fire on the tenant—a Republican Club member or sympathiser, I'm not sure which. Not one of the hail of bullets hit him, but two hit his young daughter and killed her. I had been sickened when I heard it on the news and now I went cold with fright. I didn't know precisely what time it was because it was too dark to see the bedside clock without turning on the light. But the silence outside told me it must be after midnight. That really scared me; we got very few social calls and none after nine P.M.

I leapt out of bed like I had found a corpse beside me. I doubt a corpse could have been much colder than I was just then. "Cold with fear" was a phrase I had read in thrillers but for the first time I was experiencing it from the inside. It wasn't the first time that the Troubles had touched me. When I was walking home from school one day the man in front of me had been shot dead by soldiers. When Internment was introduced in 1971 I had come under Loyalist [Protestant] sniper fire while standing beside a barricade. Our home was raided by the Brits four, five, six times. A land mine meant for a passing Army patrol had blown out our windows, brought soot down the chimney, and plunged the lights out all over the neighbourhood.

We lost our windows again when a huge car bomb exploded a few feet from our front door, seriously injuring some people standing in the street. I had been stopped, questioned, and searched by soldiers and policemen more times than I could remember.

But this was different. It was the wee small hours; it was me alone in the house and someone outside with his finger on the bell. Northern Ireland in general and Belfast in particular was in the grip of a ruthless gang war. Now I knew real fear. I was as cold as if I had just stepped from an icebox and my heart was churning blood through me at a rate I had never thought possible.

The first thing I did was tear off my pyjamas in the dark and pull on my trousers and shirt. I thought to myself that if I got shot I didn't want to be found in my pyjamas. Incredible the things you can think of at such moments. Fastening my shirt buttons, I stepped into my shoes, darted out of the bedroom, along the landing and down the stairs, swiftly but silently, for I didn't want to let on to the caller that there was anyone inside. I was already in the hallway before the bell rang a second time—*dingdong,* like millions of doorbells all over the world but the fear it struck into me was something the like of which I had never known before and have never known since. My knees were shaking like jelly, my pulse was running like an express train, and that little heart of mine—an organ of which I had scarcely ever been aware before—was beating in my ears like a punchball. Quickly and quietly like a cat—for I was always very nimble—I unlocked the parlour door and ran to the front window, hoping, praying that I would see British soldiers and/or policemen outside.

Then I would have gone to the door at once. I'm not saying I adore the security forces and I know that some members of them have been responsible for some of the worst atrocities of the Troubles, but I feel much safer opening the door to them in the dead of night than to an unknown civilian. Sure they might search the house, throw things about, ask loads of questions. The nasty ones can be very nasty and the nice ones can be very nice but nasty or nice at least you can be reasonably sure they won't shoot you dead at point-blank range. In any case, I wasn't wanted for anything so I had little to fear from them. It's the unfamiliar civilians who cause the real fear.

And my fear mounted when I slid into the chair by the window and peered through the net curtain and the space in the slats of the venetian blind. The caller was indeed an unfamiliar civilian. Although the lamp across the street was out—vandalism, I think—and the position I was sitting in afforded only restricted vision, I could make out enough of him to say with confidence that I didn't know him. Average height and weight, curly hair receding at the front—and he seemed to have a light moustache. This I detected from his profile when he turned his head to look up the street. He wore a nylon parka jacket with a fur-trimmed hood, the kind that was very much in during the seventies. Nothing sinister about that as such. I wore one myself. But I knew that it was a good coat within which to conceal a weapon, whether a handgun or an Armalite rifle with the butt broken down. Age? I'm a bad judge of ages, even in daylight, but he was somewhere between thirty and fifty.

There was a car parked at the kerb—his, I was

pretty certain, because I knew it wasn't any of those which regularly parked there. It was too dark to be sure if there was someone else in it but somehow I felt there was not. This, I thought, so far as I could still think clearly, was a good sign. The killers very seldom operated alone. Or maybe that was part of his plan—to make me think he was alone. He would know that with the feud going on nobody would answer their door without checking things out first. So maybe two or three other hoods were lying down inside the car and when I opened the door to the caller, thinking he was alone, he would dive for cover and they would spring up and open fire at me. Or maybe they were already hiding around the corner out of sight. Or maybe this caller was a diversion and the rest of his gang were already trying to break in by the back. Or maybe he was a maverick Loyalist [pro-British Protestant] gunman just looking for any Catholic victim at random. Or maybe he was just an ordinary thug intent on breaking in and ransacking the house. Or maybe he was a perfectly decent guy who had just come to the wrong door by mistake. There was no way of knowing for sure without opening the door to him and I wasn't brave enough or stupid enough, depending on how you look at it, to do that.

I was sorry I hadn't barricaded the door with tables and chairs like I knew other people were doing. It doesn't stop determined killers from getting in but it gives you a little more time to get out by the back unless, of course, they have the back covered just in case you try that. But barricading your doors has a down side too for if they lob a few petrol bombs into the back and set the whole place on fire you have to break through your own furniture before you can get out by the front.

But what was I worried about anyway? I didn't belong to the Officials or the Provos, I wasn't on any death list, I wasn't wanted by the security forces. I was just one of the many citizens who were not involved in military, paramilitary, or political activity of any kind and who just went through every day minding their own business and doing nobody any harm.

On reflection, this didn't guarantee me immunity. Lots of people had been shot for nothing except their religion—and some not even for that—some were just mistaken identities. That was one of the saddest aspects of the conflict—the many victims who took no part in violence but got snuffed out anyway. Sometimes the death dealers just got the wrong house. Malachy McGurran, I suddenly recalled—Chairman or something of the Republican Clubs—had recently issued a warning that the Provo killer squads were using outdated intelligence and were quite liable to shoot the wrong people. That had happened once already during the feud. The victim had been unfortunate enough to move into a flat vacated some weeks previously by a prominent member of the Officials. The Provos were unaware of this and shot the wrong man. The last I heard of him he was critically ill and not expected to live. Just another statistic, another few column inches in the paper but now, as every joint in me quaked with fear, I had a lot of sympathy for him. I began to gain insight into how other people, including the locally recruited security forces, must feel when a knock comes to their door in the small hours. They too must feel the clutch of fear that I now felt.

One thing for sure, though I only thought about it later, if he was a gunman he was a very patient one. His two rings had been unhurried and well spaced out—even polite—and that's not what you expect from a would-be murderer. Or was this too part of his deception? Perhaps he reckoned that if he rang persistently and aggressively he would earn my suspicion immediately and would then have to get in the hard way.

Suppose I went back to the hall and phoned the police? I would have to do it without light. I remembered police leaflets advising people how to ring the emergency services in the dark if they felt it wasn't safe to turn on their lights. That's how bad the violence was then. But we had paid the leaflets scant attention. Some people just stumble on, hoping they will never meet that kind of situation, like all those who never bother to fit a smoke alarm, thinking it will never happen to them.

I said to myself: index finger across the top row of buttons to the last, then straight down to the last—that should be 9—then press it three times and ask for the police and implore them to get here fast. Then I thought it might not be a good idea. The police had been ambushed in the past on their way to what turned out to be false alarms and they would likely think twice before driving into the heart of a Republican [Catholic] area at this hour just because somebody rang to say there was a stranger at his door.

Besides, it didn't seem very masculine. If a woman rings the police to say a stranger is at her door she might get a sympathetic hearing but a twenty-year-old guy—they might laugh at me for bringing them out for something like that. And even if I did phone them and they came promptly—which was doubtful—it would take some minutes and if the caller really was bent on murder he wasn't going to stand there much longer.

In fact, why hadn't he made his move already? Maybe I was right about him being a diversion. Maybe the real danger was developing at the rear of the house. I had better get back there and check, I thought. But wait—if I left the window I wouldn't know what the guy at the front was doing. Some people I know tell me I think too deeply about things and perhaps they are right. Maybe thinking too deeply can cause mental paralysis and leave you so you can't decide what to do. On the other hand, maybe it helps you to stay alive. The record of civil strife in Northern Ireland is not lacking in stories about people who answered knocks on their doors without a moment's hesitation and got their brains blown out.

While I was thinking all this the caller rang the bell a third time—*dingdong,* gently, quietly, with no overt hostility or menace or antagonism—but to me it was a sound that packed more fear than a thousand-pound bomb going off. I always liked peace and quiet and shunned noisy gatherings—that's one reason I grew up a loner. But just then I would have welcomed all the noises I usually detested—the drunks shouting curses on their way home from the bars, the corner boys mouthing at one another across the width of the street, the filthy joyriders screaming around in stolen cars. I would have welcomed a riot, a gun battle, or a full-scale war. Anything seemed preferable to that nerve-destroying silence of the dead hours with that stranger outside and me alone inside and that gentle *dingdong* echoing up the hall like a seductive voice beckoning me to my death.

I knew I had to do something—even if it was only run out the back and keep running—or fear would make me freeze, almost literally, on the chair where I sat. I sprang up and made for the kitchen where I pulled open the top drawer and drew out a large carving knife, sharp as a lance. I lifted the venetian blind across the kitchen window and glanced into the dark yard. So far as I could see there was no one in it and I was thankful for that. Then I went to the fireplace in the living room, lifted the poker, and ran back to the hall. Knife in one hand, poker in the other—I was well armed for an ordinary civilian who didn't have a gun and didn't want one. But who was I trying to kid? If the caller had a gun this domestic hardware wouldn't count. Still, I was pleased with myself for even having the courage to finally go to the door.

But I was still cautious and so I stole silently into the parlour again and slid once more into the chair beside the window. I was relieved—and that's an understatement—to see the stranger turning away and going back to his car. He actually closed the gate behind him—and the ill-mannered callers don't do that. Then he looked at the upstairs windows and, seeing no sign that anyone was in, got back behind his wheel. As he did so the roof light went on and I saw that he was indeed alone as I had thought. I heard his engine start up and watched him drive away.

My heart was still pounding like a steam piston out of control but I felt that the worst was over and I started breathing again. I had been short of breath many times before for I'm a keep-fit enthusiast but healthy physical exertion bears no comparison to a few minutes of concentrated fear. It took a little while for my heart to get back to anything like its normal beat and, if no other good came from that incident, at least I would never again take my heart for granted.

I went from the parlour back to the living room and from there to the kitchen where I peeked through the venetian blind again to make sure there was still no intruder in the yard.

Then I went back to the parlour again just in case the caller was pulling a fast one, driving away to throw me off guard and then returning. But, no, he was gone and the street was deserted and as quiet as a morgue. I returned to the living room once again and, feeling fairly sure that he was gone for good, turned on the light. The clock on the mantelpiece read 1:52 A.M. What in God's holy name was anybody ringing our doorbell for at 1:52 in the morning? The simplest explanation was that he was a stranger in the area and just rang the wrong door. Or maybe he was a seldom-seen relative with bad news about some member of the family circle—that would certainly account for his calling at such an hour. And it might also account for the fact that I didn't recognise him for, with one or two exceptions, I saw my relatives so infrequently that I wouldn't know them if they dropped dead in front of me. Certainly he hadn't behaved like a typical killer for the murder gangs were seldom put off by unanswered rings.

Knife still in one hand, poker in the other, I went to the inner door in the hall, unlocked it, then undid the three bolts on the outer door and unlocked it too. Warily I opened it and peeped into the street. The cool air that broke upon my face was very agreeable, just the right thing after so much tension within a confined space. I looked right, left, right, left, then laid my weapons against the doorframe and ventured as far as the gate where I looked right and left again. Not a sinner in sight. All was quiet, so quiet it might have been some other city in some other part of the world where there are no late-night killers to worry about. And it was a lovely night with the exquisite scent of late autumn in the air.

Then up the street at his usual slow crawl came a neighbour from further along the block with his little terrier on a leash—Mr . . . Mr . . . I never did know his name.

"Hello, young fella," he said. "Nice evening, isn't it?"

"Lovely," I replied. "Out for a walk, are you?"

"I walk to keep my blood pressure down."

"Just watch where you go at this time of night," I cautioned, "or you might get shot."

"You're right, you're right." He laughed as he disappeared into the darkness.

A little snatch of light conversation works wonders after so much fear. I felt myself returning to normal and then came the feelings of shame and embarrassment which I suspect most of us encounter after an unnerving experience. What had I been so worried about anyway? There was Mr. Whatever-you-call-him, three times my age, out for his constitutional, feud or no feud. It was only a stranger ringing the bell after all. I should have gone straight to the door, asked him what did he think he was playing at, knocking people up out of bed at this hour? Get lost! Clear off!

And what if he was a gunman? I would have bent

the poker over his head and buried the knife in his ribs before he got off his first shot. Most of us play John Wayne in our imagination some time or other; it compensates for lost divinity. But when the evil moment is actually upon you it can be very different. Or maybe what really scared me so much was being alone. Maybe if I had had a girl to protect I would have been brave. Perhaps when there's just yourself to care about you suffer a sense that you aren't worth fighting for. Perhaps somebody else being there can make all the difference. Being such a loner I've never been sure about that and maybe I never will be.

With my heartbeat back to normal, I withdrew inside, taking the knife and poker with me. I bolted and locked the doors, poured myself a glass of pineapple juice from the fridge, and sat down to drink it. I wondered and wondered and wondered who that caller had been and what was his business in the dead of night but I couldn't figure it. I never did find out who he was. My parents were just as baffled as I was about him when they got home.

It was a solid hour after he rang the bell before I went back to bed again and another hour before I fell back into a fitful sleep. And, although I like darkness, I can't remember a night when I was more glad to see the dawn.

While my night of anxiety had ended, not so the anxiety of others for the Republican feud was fated to send yet more people to untimely graves. Its final victim was the reputed Provo Intelligence Officer who directed the murders. Officials, who when pushed to it could match the Provos for ruthlessness all the way, walked into his favourite place of entertainment, singled him out, held him down on the floor, and pumped eight bullets into his head from three inches away.

After this, mediators were brought in to hammer out a peace deal as it was clear that neither side was winning or gaining much from the slaughter. In broad-stroke, it sounds similar to what was to happen twenty years later on a bigger scale [i.e., the current peace process].

Brenda Murphy

BELFAST

*I*t was the sectarian murder of a relative that drove Brenda Murphy, at seventeen years of age, to try to help the Republican [Catholic] cause by transporting an illegal weapon, an effort for which she was arrested and jailed. Her story tells in excruciating detail what it was like for a teenager to face years in prison—an adult prison where no allowances were made for first-time or juvenile offenders.

After paying her debt for a crime she openly acknowledges having committed, Brenda was arrested again when she was in her twenties and accused of being a member of the Irish Republican Army. She served several years in prison for the "crime" of membership in this organization, although she swears to this day that she most definitely was not a member of the IRA.

While most people would hold tremendous bitterness for the loss of so much of their youth, Brenda Murphy is undoubtedly one of the most upbeat, industrious, charming, and humorous people I've ever met. Very dedicated to her community and the fight for justice in Northern Ireland, she is well known in Belfast as a political activist who rarely takes "no" for an answer when she is trying to help someone in need. She and three members of Equality, a group to which she belongs that works to stop discrimination, were honored to be invited to personally meet

171

*with America's President Clinton when he visited Belfast
in November of 1995.*

*In addition to her community work, Brenda, now in
her forties and a mother, is a writer of some renown. Several of her stories have been published by the highly respected* Blackstaff Press *in Belfast, several others have
appeared in various anthologies, and she has a collection
of short stories that she hopes will soon be published as
well.*

Condemned

I was escorted to the holding cells, after my brief court
appearance, by two female prison officers. Flanked on
either side, each holding one of my arms, I felt like
meat in a sandwich. They told me it would be several
hours before the police had arranged an escort for the
prison van. I settled down into the corner of the cell to
wait, not speaking. I studied these two women from
head to toe. Their uniforms were royal blue. On their
heads sat three-cornered hats which had an odd, almost Napoleonic, look to them. Their thick legs and
ankles were covered by beige tights and their feet were
encased in what looked like remarkably heavy, black
lace-up shoes.

Their faces, like their tights, were also beige. The
smaller of the women in blue had a sharp pointed face
with high bony cheeks. Her eyes were very small and
seemed to be set far too widely apart. Her lips were too
thin and just a slightly darker shade of beige than her
face. Something about her face would have reminded

you of a bird, an annoying twittering, twitching bird. Not a bird who would fly gracefully, but one who would flap madly, as if it were trying to beat the air with its wings.

Her colleague in blue, although possessing the same facial colouring, looked nothing like her. Underneath the three-cornered hat was a large face, not fat, just large. Her forehead was wide, her nose was not big, but strong. Her cheek bones were broad and her eyes were normal-sized. It was her mouth which would make you look at her. Her lips were closed but the top lip sat out, well in front of her bottom lip. It gave the impression that she had a receding chin but this was not the case. When you looked closer at her mouth you could see that, although her mouth was closed, her lips met only at the corners. They were prevented from meeting by her top teeth. They were so prominent, particularly the front two, that they overshot her bottom teeth and rested on her bottom lip even while her mouth was closed. It was sad that this should be so because without those teeth she would have been a handsome woman. Not beautiful ever, but a handsome, solid woman.

For six hours we sat waiting for the police to arrange a security escort. Finally a voice shouted that we were ready to go. We walked in single file out into the open courtyard and into the prison transit. In front and behind the van I was travelling in sat police Land Rovers. They would accompany us from the police station to the prison. The windows of the van were made of smoked glass. I could see out but no one on the outside could see in. It was six o'clock in the evening—a bitterly cold evening in Belfast. Workers and last-minute shoppers hurried along streets I would probably not walk along again for many years. Their coat collars were turned up against swirling snow flurries. All these people were oblivious to the small procession of vehicles in which I was travelling. A great surge of sadness overwhelmed me. I closed my eyes and thought about the last four days and what I had been through.

I had been arrested about this time on a Monday night under the Special Powers Act.* It is an old law used only in Northern Ireland. Under these Special Powers anyone arrested can be held for up to seventy-two hours without a lawyer. The interrogations with the police are neither audio- nor videotaped. If you are charged at the end of this time you will appear in a court which has no jury. There will only be a judge to decide whether the police or the accused are telling the truth about what occurred during the interrogations.

I had heard about the beatings that were carried out in these interrogation centres. But I had never been arrested in my life and really had no idea of what actually went on after being arrested. As I had been caught with a rifle, I presumed that the need to interrogate me would be minimal. After all, I had reasoned, they had all the evidence they needed to charge me.

For the first twelve hours after my arrest I was seen by three different sets of detectives from Special Branch [for the investigation of terrorism]. These detectives asked only the questions I expected and be-

---

*The Prevention of Terrorism act, enacted in 1974, further extends police power so that a person can be held in jail for up to seven days with no access to a lawyer. This law is still in effect today in Northern Ireland.

haved in a civil manner towards me. I admitted that
the rifle was mine but refused to tell them where I got
it. I gave my name and address and asked that my parents be informed of my arrest as I was seventeen years
old and they would be worried if I did not return
home. I asked to see a lawyer even though I knew that
was not permitted. I was very nervous and more than
a little frightened but this interrogation wasn't too bad.
I thought that the stories that I had heard about interrogation centres must have been exaggerated.

The interrogation rooms that I had been brought to
were all exactly same. The rooms were fourteen
feet square, windowless, with bright fluorescent lights
burning day and night from the low ceilings. Each
room had one table in the middle and three chairs. The
fourth time I was brought to the interrogation room I
was left alone for a few moments. Then two new detectives entered the room. One was a youngish man of
about thirty-five. He was smartly dressed in a dark suit
with a white shirt and a tie. He was tall and slim. Behind him came an older man who was in his middle to
late forties. He was also wearing a suit but it was an
old suit. The knees of the trousers sagged and the
jacket had a shine to it. I could not see the waistband
of his trousers because a large beer belly hung down
over it. This older man was bald and combed some of
the hair from the side of his head across the top in an
attempt to hide his bald patch. His face was meaty and
his jawline was slack and hung in jowls. He carried a
folder which he slapped down onto the table. Then he
sat down and started to read what was in it, totally
ignoring me.

The younger detective walked around behind me

and I turned my head to follow his movements when he slapped me hard with his open hand across the back of the head. I jumped up off the chair and he grabbed me by the hair and screamed as loudly as he could that I was to sit down and under no circumstances was I to move unless he said so. I was not to look around at him and I was to answer all his questions.

Someone screaming into your ear is very painful. As he screamed his questions into me I sat silent. Every time he got no reply I got slapped on the back of the head again. Then he would scream for me to stand up and when I did he would jam his fingers, which he held out stiffly, into my back or ribs. If I bent over or put my hand instinctively up to where he had hurt me he would slap me on the head again. Then he would ask in a bewildered and angry voice what I thought I was doing standing up. When I tried to tell him that he had told me to stand up he would smack me again.

Then he decided that he would ask me questions while pushing his fingers into the bone of my chest. He used his fingers to underline each word he said. The whole time this was happening the older detective sat with his head down at the table reading the folder he had brought in with him. He could have been sitting in a quiet library on a Sunday afternoon.

This abuse from the younger detective continued for about two hours. At this stage I had taken to saying over and over again, like a mantra, "I have nothing to say, I have nothing to say."

Then there was a cough from the older man at the table. He stood up and brought his chair round to where I was seated. He put the chair right down in front of me with its back touching my knees and the seat of the chair facing out towards him. He removed his jacket and put it on the table. He rolled up the sleeves of his shirt and loosened his tie. I thought to myself, "Dear God, please don't let him start hitting me as well." He straddled the chair, throwing his leg over it the way you would sit on a horse. Then he pushed the chair tightly against my knees, forcing me to push my legs in under the chair. He put his forearms across the back of the chair and then put his face really close to mine. His nose was less than a quarter of an inch from my nose.

This intimate closeness was embarrassing to me and made me feel uncomfortable. I pulled my face away but he took my face in his meaty hand and said, "My colleague would not think it polite if you turned your face away from me, Brenda." His voice was quite beautiful. A dark brown, well-modulated voice that sounded like liquid silk. He sprayed when he spoke; a fine mist of his spittle speckled my face and lips. His breath smelled strongly of peppermint and beneath it something else. A smell of rotting meat, foul and fetid. I imagined some debris of a long-ago eaten meal stuck between his teeth and putrifying there. I felt sick.

With his beautiful voice he told me that I would tell him everything that he wanted to know. He went on to tell me that he knew that I was responsible for a cata- logue of bombings and shootings. This was totally un- true and I told him so. He looked away and his friend smacked me hard across the back of the head. I was to learn that when I denied anything to this man he would look away and I would be hit. After a while I simply refused to answer every question and every allegation. Then he started to ask if I had had sex with all the IRA men in my area. From his mouth came the most awful filth that I have ever heard in my life. His tone never changed as he described what he believed I did sexually with IRA men. I was a virgin and hearing this from a man older than my father humiliated and frightened me. I felt totally naked. I looked forward to the breaks between interviews, only to lie in the cell and dread the next interview. On the third day I was very close to breaking down. I wanted to say, "Right, okay, what do you want me to say? I'll admit to anything. Just leave me alone."

The detectives were like some sick Abbott and Costello routine, with one hitting me and the other pouring out his foul words from his foul-smelling mouth hour after hour. Of the two methods they used I could handle the violence better. I felt sexually threatened by the older man. His closeness, his spittle, his body odour totally intimidated me. When it was over and I was charged I was relieved and glad even though I knew I was going to prison.

Persistent humming broke into my train of thought. The prison officer with the prominent teeth was humming irritating snatches of hymns like "Jesus Loves the Little Children," then "Jesus Wants Me for a Moonbeam." I wondered if humming like that made vibrations run down those two enormous front teeth and did it make her bottom lip feel tingly like it did when you blew on a piece of paper over a comb. The woman with the buck teeth was tall and well built. I thought of how it would feel to be bit by those teeth. The very idea made me feel ill.

We finally arrived at the prison and I stepped stiffly down from the van. The women prison officers took an arm each and walked me across the reception yard. The walls of this yard were various shades of grey and made of enormous masonic bricks, each about two feet long. The walls were about eighteen feet high and were strung with coils of barbed wire. Bright security lights ran along the top and cameras were placed at ten-feet intervals along the walls. One camera was pointed in towards me; the other outwards. It was dark already at six in the evening and I was freezing.

We reached a thick iron door and the prison officer pressed a bell. Feet and the jangling of keys could be heard behind the door. It was opened and we stepped in. The warden who opened the door spoke to my two escorts. "Freezing, isn't it, Miss McClelland," she said.

The woman with the buck teeth replied, "It is, indeed, Miss Smith. Myself and Miss Holland will be glad of a cup of tea in the Mess."

The warden called Smith walked in front. McClelland and Holland guided me after her into a room with red tiles on the floor and pale, dirty yellow walls. On one side of the room were bath stalls with half doors on them. They walked me past these and stopped at a scrubbed wooden table. Facing the table were three small cubicles like changing rooms. These also had wooden half doors. The room was warm and smelled of carbolic and disinfectant.

"Right, who have we here?" asked the warden called Smith. The bucktoothed woman called McClelland said, "This prisoner is called Brenda Murphy," as she searched in her handbag and handed documents over to Smith. "We will leave her in your capable hands,

Miss Smith, and go to get that tea. We will see you in the wing tomorrow then, Brenda," McClelland said. But Brenda did not answer.

They left and I stood looking at the warden called Smith who was looking at the documents which McClelland had handed to her. She read them for a few moments, then lifted her head and addressed me. "Well, now. You go into that cubicle behind you, close the half door, and take off your clothes. All of them, mind. I will give you a sheet to wrap around you. Just take your clothes off and throw them over the door."

I could feel my heart hammering in my chest. "Jesus Christ, these other two will probably come back and give me a kicking."

The Warden Smith interrupted these thoughts. "Look, Brenda, nothing is going to happen to you. I write down a list of everything which you enter the prison with. You undress, put the sheet round you, and when you come out with the sheet around you, you go over and have a bath. All inmates must have a bath. When you come out of the bath I will have a fresh set of clothes ready for you."

I did not reply, nor did I move.

"Now look here, if you will not undress of your own accord I can call help down here and we will strip and bathe you by force. You don't want that, do you? Now, here's the sheet. In you go and undress." She held out a white bed sheet.

I reached slowly out and took it from her and walked to the changing cubicle. I slowly undressed. Taking off my sweater and jeans first, then wrapping the sheet around me, I wriggled out of my underwear underneath the sheet, the way you would undress at the beach. All the while my eyes never left the top of the cubicle door in case the warden would look over. When I was naked except for the sheet I sat on the built-in, slatted wooden seat that was attached to the wall behind me.

I was sure that, as a Republican [advocate of a united Ireland free of British rule], I was probably supposed to refuse to take my clothes off. But I couldn't bear the thought of being held down and stripped naked. I was too sore to bear being dragged into a bath and washed and humiliated by strangers.

"Right you are," I heard the warden say as she walked towards the cubicle. My hands were clenched into fists, holding like grim death to the sheet around me. "In you go and have a bath. I'll write a list of your clothes into the property book while you do that. And be quick now."

I walked from the cubicle to the bath stall, watching the warden over my shoulder all the time. I went in and found a large, old-fashioned bathtub which stood on claw feet. I put the plug in the bath and ran the taps. I was looking about for shampoo and soap but could see none.

The warden was at the top of the door. "Here you are," she said, handing over a towel and what looked like a two-inch-thick piece of ivory-coloured wood about three feet long.

I took both from her. "What's this for?" I asked, uttering my first words since my court appearance.

"That's soap. The male prisoners make it for us. Just break a bit off that. And you're only allowed two inches of bath water, so turn the taps off now please."

As she walked away I said, "Could I have some shampoo—my hair is really greasy."

"Shampoo. You can have shampoo when your parents bring it for you. We don't supply it so just use the soap." And with that she walked away.

I tried to break a piece of soap off the long bar but I couldn't do it. In the end, still wearing the sheet, I stepped into the bath. I took the sheet off and hung it over the bath taps so that I could grab it in a hurry. I sat with my back to the door and put the large bar of soap into the water. It was lukewarm so I turned the hot tap on.

Smith's voice rang out. "I told you, only two inches of water. Turn that tap off."

I turned it off and rubbed the face cloth vigorously along the enormous bar of soap. At last it started to give a lather. I washed my body. The carbolic soap stung my shins where the skin had been broken from the kicks I had received. My ribs hurt and there were black-and-blue finger marks on the top of both my arms.

There was a plastic jug on the corner of the bathtub which I used to scoop up the water and pour it over my hair and face. I lifted the huge bar of soap and rubbed it up and down my head. I lifted my long hair in one hand, pulled it over my shoulder, and rubbed it against the soap in an attempt to create some suds. I got very few suds but I scrubbed at my hair as hard and as quickly as I could. I called out, "I need to rinse my hair. Can I turn the water on to fill the jug?"

"No. You use what's in the bath," Smith shouted back.

"But that water's dirty," I replied.

"Just use it or don't, as you wish, but no more water!"

So I scooped up the water and poured it over my hair. I heard the warden approach so I jumped up, grabbed the sheet, and pulled it round my body just as Smith looked over the top of the stall. "Good, you're finished. Let's go," she said abruptly.

"I'm not dried yet," I said, "and I have to wash the bathtub."

"Just hurry up. I'm due my break soon. Never mind washing the bathtub. A prisoner will wash it tomorrow morning," Smith snapped.

I half dried my body. Then, wrapping the sheet tightly round me, I walked from the bath stall across the tiled floor.

I stood uncertainly in the centre of the room, hair dripping onto my shoulder.

The warden said, "Right, I have all your dirty clothing marked in the book. Do you have rings, chains, or anything like that?"

"No," I replied.

Smith continued. "Do you have any scars, bruises, or injuries?"

I said, "Yes. I'd like to see a doctor. The police beat me."

"You will see the doctor and the prison governor first thing tomorrow morning. Meanwhile, I will take note of your injuries. Have you taken, or do you take, any medication?"

"No," I replied.

Having filled in the brief medical history, Warden Smith said, "Right, come on over here and step on these scales."

"Why?" I asked. Like all fat girls, my weight embarrassed me.

"We take everyone's weight and height," Smith replied.

The scales were not the household type that you step onto and then your weight is displayed. This was an upright one where you have to move a bar along until you come to the correct weight. "About what weight are you?" Smith asked as I stepped onto the scales.

"I'm not sure, maybe nine stone," I lied, knowing I was at least a stone and a half more. [A stone equals fourteen pounds.] Smith moved the bar to nine and kept on moving it until it rested at ten and a half stone. I flushed red. I stepped off the scales and asked, "Could I have my clothes now please—I'm really cold."

"We supply you with clothes until you can wash your own or clean ones are sent in on your visit," Smith answered.

"Okay, can I have them please?" I asked again.

"Just one more thing and you can get dressed," Smith said as she walked towards me. "Just open up the sheet."

"What?" I asked, alarmed.

"Come on now," Smith said sternly, "it must be done. Everyone who comes in here must be seen."

"No," I said, "I don't see why I have to do that."

"Because the rules say you must. Now open up that sheet! It's like this—if you don't it will be removed," said Smith.

I opened the sheet and stood naked. I stared at the dirty yellow wall, my face and neck burning a bright red as this woman took a look at my naked body. Then she said, "Drop the sheet please."

I did as I was told, feeling the tears sting my eyes. This was worse than being hit and yelled at. I was seventeen, I was fat, and I felt dirty, humiliated and degraded. No one had ever seen me naked since I had reached puberty. I was ashamed of my body but I knew that even if I were as thin as Twiggy I would still feel as I did at that moment.

"Right, that's fine, you can wrap up again. Just lift each foot now, so I can see the soles," said Smith. I did so. After this Smith looked through my wet hair the way a nit nurse [a nurse who treats people for lice infestations] would and for the same reason. "Right, that wasn't so bad now, was it," said Smith.

I just looked at her. I hated this woman for what she had just done to me. I would always hate this woman. I felt that I would like another bath, a proper bath with scalding water and lots of soap.

"Right. Take these," said Smith, going to the scrubbed table and lifting a bundle of clothing from it. "What size bra are you?" she asked.

"Size thirty-eight," I said, going red again.

"Right, I'll get you one now. You go into one of those cubicles and get dressed."

I took the clothing in one arm and held the sheet tightly closed with the other. I walked into the cubicle and put down the clothes. There was a blue blouse with white spots on it and a blue cardigan. There was a pair of dark brown stockings that had been darned with red thread in about a dozen places. The skirt was of dark brown wool with an elasticized waist. There was a vest and girdle with suspenders attached to it.

The girdle was something I had only seen in films. It was a ghastly pink which people called "flesh coloured" for some reason.

Then I saw the knickers. They were thick white cotton with thick elastic at the waistband. These were enormous and there was no elastic at the legs . . . just a thick hem around each leg hole. But worse than all this was the fact that, although they had been washed and were clean, they were not new. These had been worn by someone else. I called out, "Excuse me."

"Yes, just coming. This is the only thirty-eight I can find," said Smith, handing over the bra.

"Look at these knickers. You've given me someone else's. They have been worn. Anyway they wouldn't fit me. They are far too big and there's a girdle thing here with hooks up the back. What's that for?" I asked.

"Well, now, those knickers have been boil-washed in bleach. They are perfectly clean. You don't expect to be issued with new ones, do you? New knickers are only issued when the old ones are beyond repair and have been condemned. It's the same with any other part of the prison uniform."

"Condemned," I said and went on with genuine surprise. "You condemn clothes . . . what to? The gas chamber, to be hung . . . what?"

"No, to the bin. If it can't be repaired it is condemned and thrown out. We enter it in the book. That's how we keep a check on the prison uniforms," Smith told me. "What for?" I asked. "No one is going to steal these things."

"You'd be surprised," Smith said.

"I'd be . . . astounded," I said quietly to myself. I pulled on the used, but clean, knickers. I was glad they swung between my legs like a hammock and didn't actually touch my skin. The bra was amazing—I had never seen one like it. The cups were made of what looked like small pieces of cloth sewed in ever-decreasing circles, ending in a huge point that would put your eye out. The cup on the left had been ripped off at some stage and had been sewn back in. No doubt it had been reprieved from being condemned. But, as a result of this repair, one cup was actually smaller than the other. I didn't bother complaining about it. I just squashed my left breast into it and pulled on the rest of the revolting attire.

I felt utterly ridiculous. The skirt hung on me and fell almost to my ankles and the blue spotted blouse was too tight. I took a size two in a shoe and they had none in that size so I had been given a size three which my heels slid in and out of with every step I took. I felt as if I had gone back a century . . . that it really must be 1871 instead of 1971. The clothes were so Victorian.

I shuffled behind Smith, through gates that had male officers opening and closing them. Keys jangled, hanging from skirts and trousers of the prison staff on chain-link sorts of belts.

We eventually arrived on "A" wing. It looked exactly like the picture in the poetry book, *The Ballad of Reading Gaol*. There was a slate black floor and on each side, at eight-foot intervals, set into deep doorways, were the cell doors. On the second story, which you reached by climbing a steep set of wooden stairs supported by a wrought iron frame, the layout was exactly the same. There was a catwalk right around the second story with a bridge across the centre of it. Wire had been stretched across the gap between the catwalks. It looked like heavy chicken or fencing wire.

"What's the wire for?" I asked.

Smith said, "It's called 'suicide wire.' It's to prevent prisoners throwing—"

"—I understand the word 'suicide,'" I interrupted her. I followed Smith halfway up the wing and went into what I would later discover was called "the guard room."

"One on, Miss Daly," Smith said to another warden who was sitting at a desk. I would learn that when a prisoner entered or left a wing that "one on" or "one off" would be shouted.

"New arrival, Miss Daly. All shipshape. Here's her documentation. I'll be off as I'm overdue my break," said Smith, handing the documents to the warden called Daly.

"Right you are, Miss Smith," Daly said.

"I'll see you tomorrow and no doubt for many years to come," Smith said to me over her departing shoulder.

"I'll look forward to it, pervert," I called back.

Daly stepped in between us. "Now, now, we'll have none of that. I'll take you to your cell," she said, steering me further up the wing.

She showed me into a cell which had an arched ceiling about fifteen feet high. A small, also arched window was in the thick wall close to the ceiling on the wall directly facing the door. A single bed was dead centre of the cell. Piled on the bed were a grey and black, army style blanket trimmed with red stitching, a pair of white sheets, and pillow cases. There was a white enamel basin and jug, edged with blue, and a white enamel "Po" [chamber pot], also edged in blue. A plastic, half-pint mug, a knife and fork and spoon. To the left of the bed was a small white-painted wooden locker. On it was a Bible and a stand-up cardboard thing with the prison rules written on it.

"As you are a new prisoner, you have to be locked right away. But tomorrow night you will be allowed to have association with the other prisoners until eight o'clock." Daly chattered in a friendly manner. Then she lowered her voice. "The other girls are expecting you. It was on the news that you'd been charged. They will see you at breakfast tomorrow." She meant the other Republican prisoners, but I gave no indication that I knew what she meant.

"You have had a beating," Daly went on. "I can get the medic to bring you some painkillers." I did not respond. "I'm a Catholic," she whispered. "The others will tell you I'm okay. My boyfriend's father was interned in the fifties."

"That must have been nice for him," I replied deadpan.

Seeing that she was not getting the response she had hoped for, Daly said, "I'll get the cookhouse to send you up something to eat. I know you are a little wary but you'll see I'm okay. You make up your bed and I'll be back with some food, alright?"

"Right, thank you," I replied. That seemed to please Daly who smiled and went out the door, locking it behind her.

I sat on the bed and looked around the cell. I felt like crying. I knew that [expletive], Warden Smith, was right. I would be here for many years to come.

Kevin Byers

PORTAFERRY, COUNTY DOWN

T his autobiographical story by Kevin Byers shows how the impact of the Troubles is felt far beyond the six counties of Northern Ireland. A schoolboy on his way from England to visit his grandparents in Northern Ireland for the summer, he was detained and treated like a criminal after an Irish Republican Army bomb went off in London.

Particularly since this story was written when Kevin was only eighteen, one might have expected it to include anger and a certain amount of invective against the heavy-handed British authorities. But Kevin maturely refused to see the conflict in black-and-white terms and included an event that gives the story an enigmatic, ambiguous ending.

The Leaving of Liverpool
(Written at age eighteen)

"**A**re you, or have you at any time been, a member of an illegal organization?" The Special Branch officer yawned as he began reading from the sheet of questions for the third time. The first time I had laughed nervously after each answer but now I cried them out.

"No, I've told you . . ."

"Where were you at two o'clock this afternoon?"

"On the train to Liverpool," I sighed.

The officer looked at me with disgust and threw his clipboard down on the desk between us. "Alright, pal, we'll leave you to the boss. It looks like the Bridewell [prison] for you tonight."

He walked out and left me alone in the office. It was the first time I'd had to think since they had taken me from the docks to the police station. I had joined the queue to board the ship for Belfast. I was looking forward to spending my summer holiday with my cousins in Ireland. I was fifteen and making the journey alone for the first time.

I noticed two men walking down the line, pointing out some of the passengers to each other. One of them stopped and pulled a man out of the line. I was watching him being taken to a white mini [small car] on the dockside when I felt a finger tapping me on the arm. Before I realized what was happening, I was in the white mini with the other passenger and the two Special Branch men who were driving us through the damp and dreary backstreets of Liverpool.

We had been taken to different rooms when we arrived. As I sat on my own staring at the walls, I wished that my unknown companion was there to tell me why we were being questioned. Perhaps he didn't know either.

The walls were covered in the shiny blue emulsion that they use in schools and hospitals and it was flaking and peeling in large patches. The desk was old and scratched and an ancient black telephone sat in the middle of an empty out-tray.

I could see the clipboard with my questionner's notes and I wondered if I had time to take a look at what he had written. No . . . what if they were watching me? Perhaps that was what they wanted me to do to prove I was guilty of whatever it was they thought I had done? I wanted a cigarette but I didn't know whether that was allowed, so I just sat waiting for the next move. I began to wonder if I really was guilty of some crime committed in a moment of mental blackout. I laughed at the thought but stopped myself. The idea that I was being watched had not left me.

I was snapped back to reality by the appearance of a tall, bald-headed man in the doorway. "Well, son," he said softly, "you're a bit young for all of this, aren't you?"

"Yes, I . . . I suppose I am." The blood shot to my head and my cheeks coloured as the fear that I might have just incriminated myself further took hold of me. This must be the "boss" who my previous questionner had mentioned. He gave me a reassuring smile so I decided to ask the question that had been nagging me: "Am I . . . under arrest?"

"No, no lad," he said soothingly. "You're simply in for routine questioning under the Prevention of Terrorism Act." His voice had slipped abruptly into a cold, official tone with the last few words and I felt goosebumps appear on the back of my neck. He seemed to sense my fear and immediately used the opportunity.

"We want to know all about this afternoon. Now, come on, lad, it'll be better for you and all of us if you tell us the truth now."

I looked around the room in desperation, as if expecting to find someone there to help me. I was totally alone for the first time in my life. I suddenly felt guilty again. "I don't understand," I finally whimpered.

He looked at me for several minutes, staring me straight in the eyes. Eventually, he sat down. "You really don't know, do you?"

"No, honestly, I wish I did," I said, seeing a glimmer of hope and trying to sound as young and innocent as I could.

He threw down the newspaper that he had been carrying and I immediately saw the headline: "IRA Bomb in London Hotel." My eyes seemed to blur and I couldn't read anymore. "Oh, Christ, no, you can't really think that I had anything to do with this?"

He looked me in the eye again and his fatherly reassuring tone returned. He asked me my phone number and, when I told him, he moved toward the office door.

"Was there anyone . . . hurt?" I called to him, meaning to say "killed" but the word would not come out.

"No, lad," he confided. "It's just as well for you that there wasn't or you might never have got as far as me."

He walked out of the room to the next office and within seconds I could hear him talking on the phone.

"Yes, he's alright . . . nothing to worry about . . . just routine. . . . Now, you can confirm that he left London on the lunchtime train from Euston? Right, thank you very much. He'll be on his way soon."

At these last words I felt a rush of relief. I looked at my watch and realized how long I had been there. The ship would be sailing soon and the thought of being stranded in a city I had come to hate filled me with a new fear.

When the officer came back in, he picked up the receiver of the old black telephone on the desk. My mind was reeling so that I only took in the last few words. ". . . right, Jim, hold it for another ten minutes. This one's clean. Did the other one go on board yet? Good. It looks like whoever did it knew better than to come through this way. My guess is they'll lay low for a while. Right, good night, Jim."

He quickly brought me down to where the white mini was waiting to drive me back to the ship. My luggage was on the back seat where I had left it. A piece of material was just visible where one of the cases had been carelessly closed. As we drove back to the docks, I vowed to avoid Liverpool for the rest of my life.

Walking towards the gangway, I felt that everyone on the ship's decks was watching me. They knew who I was and where I had been. My ticket was hastily checked and the gangway removed as soon as I was on board the ship. I went straight to the cafeteria for a cup of coffee and the cigarette that I had been longing for all evening. I carefully avoided everyone's eyes. After a while, I became aware of someone standing beside me. I recognized him as soon as I looked up.

"Hello there, so they let you out as well then. I knew they would. The bastards were just trying to put the wind up you." He sat down and I smiled at him with the relief of having someone to talk to who had shared the same experience. We had been total strangers a few hours earlier when we were taken to the police station together but now I felt a strong affinity with him.

"I'm glad to see that you got out as well," I said, meaning every word of it.

"Who, me?" He smiled. "They let me go after five minutes . . . as soon as I showed them this." He waved a piece of paper in front of me. "It tells them that I was just let out of Long Kesh [maximum security prison outside Belfast also called The Maze] a week ago and was over in England for a job interview. I had no trouble with them . . . and I didn't get the job either!"

We both laughed and then we went up on deck and sat on a wooden bench. By one o'clock I had told him my whole story and England was just a few fading lights in the darkness.

"You can call me Gerry by the way," he said.

"And I'm Kevin . . ."

He held up his hand to stop me from saying more.

"First names are enough for us, Kevin." He spoke gently but firmly. I felt a strange fear that I could not understand. He smiled, as if he knew what I was thinking, and walked over to the railings.

"All the same, Kevin," he said after a pause, "they're terrible stupid, falling for a bit of paper like this." He tore the paper up and dropped the pieces onto the water below.

Alison Östnas

BANGOR, COUNTY DOWN

*O*ne of four children, Alison Östnas was born in Belfast
in 1956. Her father was an Army officer and her mother a
college lecturer. The family lived in an area that was rela-
tively undisturbed by the Troubles, Alison says, but her
extracurricular activities were curtailed and her journeys
to and from school at Victoria College in Belfast were delayed by riots from time to time. She especially remembers
that during the Workers' Strike in 1974 young boys of
twelve and thirteen, armed with sticks, barricaded roads
and prevented people from going to work.

Asked what inspired her in 1992 to write this, the only
story she has written, Alison said, "I wanted people to
know how ordinary families were at the mercy of armed
groups who always had the advantage of surprise."

Unwelcome Callers

I was eighteen, in my first year as a student nurse. My
mother and I were relaxing after a hard day. Our dog,
dozing at our feet, suddenly pricked up his ears at the
sound of crunching gravel. The bell rang and I opened
the door, to be confronted by two youths unknown to

me. The smaller of the two stepped forward and thrust a revolver into my chest. "We've come for Tom's gun," he said, "and we know it is here."

My heart sank. If they knew so much, where was Tom, my policeman brother? Was he being held in some terrorist stronghold until this mission had been accomplished?

Meanwhile, I was pushed into the sitting room where our brave protective dog was cowering in the corner. The gunman ordered his mate to "go upstairs and get it." He headed straight for my brother's room and soon we could hear drawers being pulled out, contents scattered, cupboard doors wrenched open, and carpets ripped back.

Downstairs, we had time to study the other young terrorist. He was a tight little chap—tight lips, tight curls, tight jeans—but his tightly clenched hands could not control the tremor in the fingers clutching the gun. To ease the tension I had the crazy impulse to offer him a cup of tea. Instead, I asked him whether his mother knew what he was doing. He looked very uncomfortable and said that it was better to "keep the oldies in the dark." His mother was probably in her thirties.

Just then our discourse was interrupted by his mate, a big, lumbering lad with a rather vacant expression. If brawn should be required, he would supply it. He confessed, apologetically and rather desperately, that he "couldn't find it," and was dispatched upstairs again to search the other bedrooms. My mother and I exchanged a concerned glance, knowing that a hat box on top of her wardrobe contained spare ammunition. More bangings and clatterings ensued, the top was removed from the lavatory cistern [toilet tank], and the contents of the airing cupboard [for linen and clothing] came floating downstairs.

Meanwhile, my mother's car keys were demanded, the phone wires pulled out, and instructions given regarding the time lapse to be observed before reporting the incident. Once more the lumbering lad came downstairs, worry written all over his face. He had failed on his first "job." The boss was very angry but decided to settle for my brother's police uniforms which could be used in bogus road blocks.

Eventually the sidekick came down, draped in beautifully pressed trousers and tunic, a night helmet at a rakish angle on his head, and a truncheon [nightstick] under one arm. Over the other arm hung a pair of binoculars. Outraged, my mother blurted out, "You can't take those. They belong to my husband!"

Meekly and apologetically, the trainee terrorist handed them over. He had not yet learned that hard men never say sorry. Emboldened by this small triumph, my mother requested the return of her house keys, and, to her surprise, they were detached from the ring and handed over!

At last, the intruders were ready to leave and, luckily for them, their car started.

Our first act was to examine the phone. It was well and truly disconnected but would this alone constitute grounds for replacement? My mother had been agitating for months to have the old-fashioned, heavy black instrument replaced by a modern streamlined one, colour to be chosen from a limited range. Perhaps a short, sharp tap would do the trick? I fetched the hammer.

My brother arrived home later, unaware of the

drama, to find the house surrounded by soldiers and police and his mother and sister poring over jigsaws of noses, foreheads, and hairlines while the features of our callers were still clear in our minds. To his great relief, his revolver was still in its ingenious hiding place.

There were several sequels to the incident. Our "semi-detached" [duplex] neighbours greeted us rather frostily next morning with mutterings about late-night parties and comings and going at all hours of the night.

My father, who had left on the morning of the "visitation" to return to Scotland where he was working at the time, noticed two men following him onto the platform of the local railway station. They were probably ensuring that there would be no male presence in the house.

And a few months later, my brother's uniforms were discovered during a police raid on a Belfast pub. The name tapes were still sewn into each garment and the pub manager was now in trouble.

About three years later, we learned that our uptight terrorists had soon gained confidence and graduated to more serious assignments. In fact, they were currently up on a murder charge. We were lucky to have been involved in one of their first jobs.

On the plus side, our new phone, in our chosen colour, arrived next day!

Lisa Burrows

Lisa Burrows says her childhood wasn't much affected by the Troubles, but she does remember having to be especially wary of bombs at Christmas time. "I remember the hotel near our house was bombed—devastated and in ruins," she says, "but it was accepted as normal, a day-to-day happening . . . the shootings and bombings were so frequent that it was just accepted."

In the following account of her coming of age, Lisa shows how she gradually came to be more and more accepting of Catholics as she grew older and how, even though a romantic relationship was forbidden her, she was able to build a close friendship with a Catholic boy.

Neil
(Written at age seventeen)

→>–<←

You know how it is. When you're eleven or twelve, impressionable and a Protestant, the Catholics are always the bad guys. Then you move on—thirteen, fourteen—you don't have much contact with them. They're still bad, but more of a curiosity. Fifteen—

your best friend goes out with one, loses her virginity to him, and you begin to accept them more. Then she falls out with him and you're back to the eleven- or twelve-year-old stage. Once you're in college you're basically outnumbered and all the old prejudices have to be left at home with your teddy bear. You enter into a friendly world with Catholics, ignoring what it says on television about the latest bombing or shooting, forgetting the things your parents told you about "them ould Micks."

Sixteen. Sweet sixteen, the magical age. What is it about the teenager that makes the older generation cry, "Oh, no, not the teenager—it's a curse!" Being a teenager is tough. There's the "Does he or does he not like me?" stage, the "I'm not a baby, let me curse, smoke, drink, go out with my friends stage," the "Let me dress how I want and express myself" stage. But try including any of these stages with something major like . . . moving house for instance. Not a good idea.

I was sixteen when I left my old school and all my old friends behind to go to Downpatrick College of Further Education. My first day was disastrous. I knew nobody, had to take a strange bus to a strange place whose doors I'd darkened only once in August. Worst of all, I had to hang about with myself. I'm normally a gregarious person and horribly conservative; so, as normally I loathe changes, you can imagine what my first day was like. Come Monday, I began to fit in more, find my niche, and stay in it. Tuesday, I'd gone to dinner with two girls. They were Catholics. Wednesday, I pleased my mother and fell in with some Protestants whom I stuck tightly to and whom I am still with. College gradually improved and now, eight months after I first got here, lonely and frightened, I feel I fit in.

After two months we had to move house. We had sold our house on the day my GCSE [college exams] results came out. We were moving to Ardglass, to a brand new house which was supposed to be built and finished for June 1994, September 1994, November 1994, December 1994, January 1995 . . . It was eventually finished in March 1995—nine months late. We had to be out of our old house in the second week of September. Since rented houses were too expensive—and it was only to be for a month, two at most—we moved in with my Granny at her house in Killyleagh. We were to live there six months, during which I discovered that Catholics could be friendly and that I as a Protestant could be accepted by them for who I was, not what I was. It was especially surprising when one took me under his wing, so to speak, and went out of his way to make me welcome.

There were no Protestants in Killyleagh for me to hang about with. In fact, the girl I did hang about with was and is going steady with a Catholic. This left me on my own pretty much as she was always with him and I had no wish to play gooseberry [chaperone, or an unwanted party to a couple]. So what did I do when I was bored in the evenings? I certainly didn't sit in the house! I called for Neil. Neil was the only guy in Killyleagh whom I could confide in. Sure, everyone was friendly enough, but Neil had that something which prompted me to see more and more of him. It got to the stage where everyone thought we were, to use an old-fashioned phrase, walking out together. It was actually rather funny because some of the girls thought we were an item and were jealous. This led them to ignore me. It's not even as though Neil's the best-looking fellow among the guys—because he's not—but he's definitely the easiest to talk to and the friendliest. Everyone knows Neil. So there I was, a newcomer and I had snitched the nicest guy from right under the residents' noses—no wonder they all whispered about me. But they'd all got the wrong idea! After my initial shyness, which I soon got over, I was always with "the guys," as they were known. I ran with the pack nearly every night, except the nights I was working. There were many times when I guess I could have been raped. I mean frequently there was just me and around six to ten boys. That makes me sound like a slut and I'm not, but that's just the way it was. The guys respected me and I was an unknown quantity too, I guess, so no one ever tried anything. I was also under Neil's protection and his word seemed to matter a great deal within the group.

I was still hanging around with Neil and company. My parents made it clear that they didn't approve and Granny nearly had a canary the night that Peter and Neil called at the door for me. Mum and Dad definitely didn't encourage this but they didn't forbid me from seeing them. As Daddy said, "If I say that you aren't allowed to see them then you'll just be all the more determined to do it. So you can continue your relationships provided that you don't go out with one of them. I don't want to see you hurt."

I was always slipping down the road to see them. As

Mum said later, I didn't think about anything else, didn't have time for anything else. The crunch came when by accident Mum read part of an old jotter I keep my diary in. It told her that I was "cracked" on Neil. . . .

"So what?" I hear you say. But for me this was an invasion of my privacy and it had a profound effect on me. After my six-month sojourn in Killyleagh, moving house again was a big wrench. I must have been weepy for about a week after it. Mum thought that when we had moved I would forget about "McArdle." Not so. I was still infatuated of course. Every Thursday I went "home" on the Killyleagh bus to Granny's house just to see him. Every Sunday I was making excuses to go down to the Priory to him.

It would have made my life so much easier if we had been of the same religion. The peace process had begun at the same time as I had moved to Killyleagh, but it had no effect on attitudes. Why do Catholics and Protestants hate each other? Is it the inbred fear that comes with hatred? Always there's the "them" and "us" factor. Why should religion have to matter? The whole world seems split by religion: Bosnia, Iran/Iraq, Ireland. . . . Why do we as a people always see our opinions to be correct? From an early age we are told that it is not what is outside a person but what is inside that counts. Why does this not seem to matter where religion is concerned?

I seem to have portrayed my family in an awful light. My parents tolerate the relationships and Granny helps me escape down the street sometimes. But what of the rest of my family? What do they think? Do I want to know?

I still continue my relationships in Killyleagh. Sure

I get strange looks and all sorts of comments, but I don't really mind anymore. You could say that I'm conditioned to it now. My aunt is forever putting in barbed comments about my friends and because her daughter is going with a staunch Protestant she thinks that she is in the right. There's no problem with her daughter going into town to meet him and no problem with her going off with him for the whole evening, yet I have to beg, plead and cajole to stand fifteen minutes on the street corner with Neil.

There are times when I think that Neil isn't worth the hassle, but other times I get determined and ask myself why should religion have to matter. Surely it's the person's psyche that matters. For example, I called down for Neil on Sunday, after obtaining permission from Mum to go down the street for fifteen minutes. Neil was on his way out so he answered the door coat-in-hand. We went down to the hut and I was greeted vociferously by everyone. When my allotted time was up I had some time alone with Neil when he walked me home. Now that was the Neil I know—friendly, funny but intimate. On Tuesday I met everyone again at the bus stop. I met a different Neil then—even the rest of the guys were different. Indifferent, trying to act the smart ass. . . . Only Neil was quiet and begged me with his eyes to put up with the teasing. On days like Sunday when we're down at the hut or on our own, I know that the hassle I sometimes go through is worth it. On days like Tuesday I begin to wonder.

I'm not allowed to go out with Neil. I respect my Dad's opinion on that score, but the attraction is there between us. I realise that here in Northern Ireland relationships between Catholics and Protestants are strained. But should religion affect how you view a person? Surely not. However, old prejudices run deep.

Religion? Two differing ways of worshipping God. Does He really mind how we worship him? The most important thing is that we do it.

Stephen Hoey

ENNISKILLEN, COUNTY

FERMANAGH

Sometimes the gap between Protestants and Catholics can be bridged in simple and unexpected ways, as Stephen Hoey indicates in this autobiographical story. When he almost accidentally learned that he had much in common with Catholic boys and enjoyed their company, he took a radical turn away from the sentiments of many if not most in the Protestant community. Today Stephen says that most of his friends are Catholics and that, in fact, his best friend is from a Catholic family.

The Road Rats Cometh

"There's fourteen Fenians [slang for Nationalist Catholics] in the morgue."

So said D with an air of subdued delight in his voice as he ran up to me that Saturday morning in June.

D was one of the younger boys on my estate [housing project] and prone to exaggerate but even by Northern Ireland standards this was big news. "What happened?" I asked. "What's going on?"

"Last night," he went on enthusiastically, "at the dance in the marquee [entertainment tent] there was a riot, I tell you, and there's fourteen Catholics dead and fifty of them in the Erne Hospital."

Fourteen of my archenemies dead? Loads more hurt? Sounds okay to me, I thought. I hope the one who beat me up last Christmas is among the fatalities. I must watch out for his name on the casualty list in next week's paper.

I kicked my motorcycle into stuttering, two-stroke life. I'll go for a spin downtown and try to find out more about last night's trouble. It must have something to do with that bike gang who rode into town last night. Who were they? Where did they come from? And how come they killed so many Catholics?

I rode around town which, even on a busy Saturday morning, doesn't take very long in Enniskillen. My eyes were peeled for the high security presence which follows incidents like this. But there was nothing. I rode on to the scene of the alleged massacre but there was nothing much there either—just some broken fencing, one or two sightseers, and an empty marquee. So what did happen?

Over the next few days the true story came out. The biker gang was from Lurgan, a town fifty miles away. They had come to the dance at the marquee, by now an annual event, to hear a rock band and have a bit of a wild time. Owing to some high spirits on their part, some non-biking locals had taken offence and a major brawl had broken out. Nobody had died—no Catholics, no Protestants. There were some injuries including, unfortunately, the loss of one biker's eye but certainly no death toll of fourteen. Exaggerations abound in the teenage mind.

Deaths or not, this was a major event to a seventeen-year-old aspiring Hell's Angel and to confine its contemplation to the boys from my estate seemed to be a bit of a waste. But who else could I discuss it with from a biker's point of view?

The answer was to come the following Thursday afternoon. I was sitting on my bike outside the local bike shop which was, and still is, the meeting place for anyone on two wheels. A purple Yamaha pulled up alongside me. But this was no ordinary Yamaha because when its rider removed his helmet I saw he was a Catholic!

I tried to casually finish my cigarette without appearing to rush things, put on my helmet, and prepared to go.

"What about Friday night?" he asked, straight at me. "Heavy scene or what?"

I switched off my ignition partly through shock, partly through having flooded the engine in my eagerness to be gone. "Aye, it was some night!" I answered. "Were you there?"

"No," he went on, "I just went down on Saturday morning after I'd heard about it. I heard there were loads of people killed and injured but the whole thing was blown out of all proportion."

We discussed the night's events at length and, when I finally did ride away, my head was spinning faster than my motor. Here was I, some Protestant biker rebel without a clue having just shared a conversation and a cigarette with a Catholic who was quite possibly a real rebel with a clue.

Well, things changed dramatically after that first encounter. The next time I met Michael at the bike shop he was with some of his friends and we talked some more about that Friday night. Then a few of my friends joined in and before too long we all began calling at each other's houses in different parts of town—parts where, prior to that, we wouldn't have dared venture.

Shortly afterwards we even formed our own bike club. "Road Rats" it said on the colours that we proudly wore. We were, perhaps, the first cross-community organisation by the youth, for the youth, in Enniskillen. We, of course, didn't see it that way. We just wanted to be outlaws, man!

Over the next few years many lifelong friendships were formed—not only between us riders but with each other's families, friends, and neighbours—and we all agreed that we should have gotten together much sooner.

Looking back now, we were just boys trying to become men and, thankfully, we did it well enough, I think, because, even though most of us have sold our motorcycles years ago, we can still drink a beer together whenever the opportunity arises and we can talk about those biking years. And in the same breath we can discuss the politics and problems that still exist in this country that we share. We can do it in a way that does not offend each other nor, hopefully, anyone else.

Sometimes I like to think that it was just our passion for motorcycles that brought us together then—that we were some special breed, that we had our own colours to nail to the mast so we didn't need anyone else's. Sometimes I like to think that, for me at least, it was the example set by my parents. After all, it was they who had encouraged me to buy a bike in the first place and to always respect the views of others.

But deep down I hope that it was something more. I hope that all boys to men can do what we did, that they can all find something—anything—that can break the ties that bind and make them start talking.

THE ISRAELI/
PALESTINIAN
CONFLICT

Damascus

LEBANON

SYRIA

GOLAN
HEIGHTS

Haifa

Sea of
Galilee

Plain of Sharon

Jezreel Valley

*Beit She'an
Valley*

Jordan R.

Mediterranean Sea

WEST

Nablus

Ramat Gan
Tel Aviv
Jaffa

Petah-Tikva

Beit El
Ramallah

Amman

BANK

Jerusalem
Bethlehem

Dead

Gaza

Hebron

GAZA
STRIP

Sea

ISRAEL

JORDAN

Negev

EGYPT

⬚ Area occupied by Israel
since the 1967 Six-Day War

Prior to the founding of Israel
in 1948, all of the territory that
is now Israel was Palestine.

0   miles   25

0   kms   25

Introduction

The struggle between Israeli Jews and Palestinians—two ethnically and culturally distinct peoples—although one of the most complex and longstanding conflicts in the world, is fundamentally about one thing: both peoples claim the same land as their homeland and, to varying extents, both want to govern it as *they* see fit. Add to this the fact that people of various ethnicities, including Druze and Bedouin Arab, also occupy the same land, and it becomes even more understandable that the efforts of numerous world leaders have yet to bring peace to this very troubled land.

As the writers in this section so poignantly describe, Israeli and Palestinian children grow up feeling that they are destined for conflict with their neighbors from the day they are born and that there is little they or anyone else can do about it. To be born an Israeli Jew or a Palestinian is to be heir to an ethnic identity one is expected to defend at all costs. Until Yasser Arafat and Yitzhak Rabin's famous White House handshake, in 1993, sealing the Declaration of Principles designed to lead to a permanent peace accord, there was virtually no hope of an Israeli-Palestinian peace.

Today, however, despite tremendous hurdles to peace that have arisen subsequent to the signing of the

Declaration of Principles—numerous assassinations, massive bombings with tremendous loss of life, threats to sacred sites, and the continuing struggle over the future of Jerusalem—there is at last a possibility that the writers in this book will see peace in their lifetimes.

From Palestinian refugee camps in the West Bank and the Gaza Strip to Jewish kibbutzim in Israel and the occupied territories, from the Old City of Jerusalem to Ramallah to modern Tel Aviv, Israeli Jews and Palestinians tell us the story of their youth—sometimes happy, more often sad, and all too frequently horrific.

Still, no matter what their ethnic identity, how much and how long they and their families have suffered, and how extreme their differences, the authors of these courageous autobiographies most often reveal a deep longing for peace.

They do not, however, pretend to kiss and make up. Although often expressing a desire for understanding and reconciliation, they accuse and assign blame: they express hate, anger, fear, grief, humiliation, despair, and the desire for revenge. Nevertheless, if they can suspend judgment for a time and hear each other I think they have a chance of bringing their painful, century-long conflict to an end. The first step, no matter how difficult, is for them—and all of us—to listen to the stories of one another's lives.

Readers will note that some of the authors of the autobiographical writings in this section have chosen to use pseudonyms. Although none were questioned about their reasons for doing so, it is reasonable to assume that they felt a need to protect themselves and their families from retaliation, which, unfortunately, is a pervasive threat for Israelis and Palestinians alike.

All stories have been edited for length, common English usage, spelling, punctuation, etc., except those few that have previously been published in English. (Variant spellings have been retained for certain place names, etc.) I have added explanations of words and concepts I think readers may not be familiar with and placed them in brackets.

There are wounds and losses, pain and suffering, unrealized potential when young people grow up in near-constant conflict. But there are also strengths and wisdom born of growing up in conflict, and I, for one, would never call the writers in this book "victims," "damaged," or "dysfunctional." I would call them experts in coping with some of the most difficult situations human beings can face. And I would call them courageous for being willing to share their secret pain and sorrow, defeats and triumphs, here.

More than anything, I would say I have learned that so long as we teach young people to rely on their ethnic identities to tell them who they are and who they should become, we will have violent conflict. I believe that ethnic identity is a construction, a concept that is taught to us when we are young, and that it is only when we learn to formulate an identity quite apart from ethnic, sectarian, racial, national, and religious heritage that we will come to have enough understanding of each other to live together. Until that day comes, let us listen to each other's stories and teach our children the meaning of equal opportunity and justice.

LAUREL HOLLIDAY
1997

Gunter David

*G*unter David was born in Berlin, just as Hitler was rising to power. He and his family fled to Paris in 1933, and then, when he was five years old, they moved to Tel Aviv. Just before the creation of the State of Israel, in 1948, David came to the United States to study journalism and acting. Over the course of twenty-five years he was a writer for several major city newspapers including The Baltimore Sun, *Philadelphia's* Evening Bulletin, and The New York Times, *host of a daily radio program on consumer affairs, a foreign correspondent who covered the Yom Kippur War for the* Philadelphia Daily News, *and a contributor to several national magazines.*

A resident of Philadephia for the last twenty-five years, and married to his wife Dalia for forty-five, Gunter David is father to three children and grandfather to five. He is currently in private practice as a psychotherapist in Philadelphia and devoted to his new career as a fiction and creative nonfiction writer. He received first prize in the literary short story category in the 1997 annual Philadelphia Writers' Conference.

In this story David explores the hard choice he had to make as a teenager between his desire to remain in his homeland and his desire to realize his dreams.

Going to Jerusalem

+>-<+

"**D**on't sit by the door. You could take a bullet," my father warned me.

"Go with God," my mother said. I felt her tears on my neck, there, in front of the apartment house, under the tall, bare tree, its brown leaves scattered on the sidewalk by the cold December wind.

"Take care of yourself," my father said. We shook hands. I buttoned my coat and walked to the corner of Shenkin. The bus to downtown came in a moment, and I quickly turned and waved. They waved back, holding on to each other, alone together.

I was going to Jerusalem. Beyond Jerusalem lay America: Times Square, Broadway, Hollywood, palatial homes, swimming pools, cars, nice clothes, malt shops, jitterbug, jazz. That was America to me.

I was eighteen years old.

The dispatcher at the cab stand on Rothschild, just off Allenby, waved me into the back of the big, black car. It was empty, smelling of tobacco. Two jump seats were unfolded, awaiting passengers. I settled into the middle seat in the rear. I knew it was selfish, but I wanted to be safe. At least, as safe as possible.

I put my hand inside the breast pocket of my jacket to make sure the new British Passport 224866, issued by the government of Palestine, was safe. Soon it would contain a visa granting me entry to the United States.

No war. No Arabs. No shooting. No bombs.

* * *

I'd wanted to live in America ever since I started going to the movies. I used to imagine all of America as one big movie set. Chaim Rosoff, who lived next door to our third floor walk-up in Tel Aviv, called America the "Goldene Medine," the Golden Land. "It's where dreams come true," he used to say.

Soon I would dream there too.

The dispatcher interrupted my thoughts.

"Move over," he commanded. "Sit by the door. Let the girl sit in the middle."

"But I was here first. I want to sit in the middle."

"What's the matter? You're too scared to sit by the door?" He laughed, a dark, swarthy man with thick eyebrows and golden teeth.

"If he's scared, let him sit in the middle." A husky voice announced an attractive girl, about my age. Her cheeks were red from the wind, her dark eyes shining with laughter.

I moved to the door.

In short order, the rest of the passengers entered the cab. The girl next to me placed a bag in her lap, extracted two knitting needles attached to yarn, twisting snake-like from the bag, and began to knit. She shook her long, light brown hair free of her jacket. A bearded young man, wearing a skull cap, sat on her other side and began reading. Two middle-aged women occupied the jump seats, and a young couple sat up front. No one spoke.

The driver was the last to arrive. When he turned around, our eyes met.

"Avraham!" I exclaimed.

He smiled.

"Since when are you driving a cab?" I asked.

"Why would you be going to Jerusalem?"

"I . . . well . . . I'm going on an errand. For my father."

"I'm filling in for the driver. My sick uncle."

"Yaallah, let's go!" shouted the dispatcher. Avraham turned the key in the ignition. We lurched ahead.

Avraham mustn't find out why I was going to Jerusalem, I thought. He mustn't find out that I was leaving for America. I knew what he would say. He'd say, "You're a quitter. How can you leave us behind? Your *chevre* [community], your friends, your people? How can you walk out on this fight for our independence? In a few months we'll have our own state. For the first time in two thousand years. And you won't be part of it."

I knew how I would respond. I'd say, "There'll never be peace with Arabs. There'll always be killing. I live only once. I want to live where there's peace. Where I can get somewhere. I have a right to live my life my way."

We had had these discussions before, Avraham and I, when we were in high school. He was a Zionist, born in the Land of Israel. I was born in Germany, and my family fled from Hitler. "Sands, flies, and Arabs," my father said a few months after we arrived in Palestine.

I could hear the sounds of voices and running feet that awakened me one night in 1936 when I was six years old. My parents were carrying blankets and pillows out of our apartment in North Tel Aviv. From my window I saw flames, like moving golden sheets, illuminating the southern horizon, toward Jaffa. Scores of men, women, and children were huddled in the open red poppy fields in front of the house. People were bringing them food and supplies.

"The Arabs attacked Jews on the border of Jaffa and Tel Aviv," my father explained when he returned. "They shot them and set their houses on fire." He sat down on a chair in the kitchen and wiped his face with a handkerchief. "I was just there this afternoon. . . ."

It was the start of the Meoraot, the Disturbances, that were to last until the outbreak of World War II. Many a night I would hear the crackling of gun shots and scamper under my bed. In the morning I would examine the outside walls for bullet marks.

I thought of it all as we moved forward, down Allenby and other city streets, to the Central Bus Station. There we joined a convoy of buses, taxis, and private cars. Rumors had it that members of the Haganah, the Jewish underground, accompanied the convoys for protection against attacks by the Arabs. Scores of young men milling about alongside vehicles seemed to give credence to the rumors. I had been briefly one of them, but received a medical discharge after being diagnosed with a heart murmur. Now I would be protected by them—I who was leaving them behind.

The flat lands outside Tel Aviv whizzed by, apartment houses soon giving way to Jewish settlements surrounded by wire fences and guard towers. The road to Jerusalem lay before us, gradually twisting and climbing up the mountains of Judea. Stone houses of Arab villages, carved into the mountain sides, appeared after a while. Arabs and Jews lived practically side by side. They might as well have been deserts apart.

Avraham drove steadily, at a fast clip, somewhere in the heart of the convoy, a bus in front and another in back of us. No need to linger in enemy territory. We'd been traveling for about an hour when one of the women in the jump seats began eating a sandwich.

The girl next to me looked at her and laughed. "Some people always think they'll starve," she said to no one in particular.

The woman turned around.

"You know, sweetheart, you're much too skinny. I bet your mother tells you that you don't eat enough."

"My mother's dead," the girl said quietly. "Killed when Arabs attacked our kibbutz."

"I'm sorry." The woman reached out and touched the girl's hand. "Forgive me."

A sign by the side of the road proclaimed, "Latrun. Military Installation. Government of Palestine."

The bus ahead of us slowed down. The woman and the girl settled back in their seats. Avraham stopped the car.

"Roadblock," he explained.

From my window I saw British soldiers fanning out among buses and cars, banging on doors, shouting, signaling drivers to stop. Two of them, one on each side of our taxi, opened the doors up front. The polished shotguns on their backs glistened in the sun. The soldiers examined the faces of the driver and the couple. Then they looked on the floor of the car. They slammed the doors shut and opened the back doors.

The man with the beard continued reading, never acknowledging their presence. The young woman knitted as she had been doing since we left Tel Aviv. Were they looking for weapons, I wondered, or for the Hagana? Someone from the Irgun, or the Stern Gang— the other Jewish underground organization?

"Step out, please," one of the soldiers told the passengers in the jump seats. The two women leaned on the backs of the seats for support, the one still holding her partly eaten sandwich. When the women had left the taxi, the soldiers examined the floor. They folded back the jump seats. They looked at the floor under our feet. I felt exposed. They looked at our faces. I had nothing to hide, yet I could feel my heart racing.

The soldiers backed out. The women returned. The soldiers slammed the doors shut.

"*Mamzerim*," [bastards] murmured the girl next to me. "At least they could have flipped back the jump seats."

"Quiet," said the woman with the sandwich. "Don't make trouble."

"Why don't they go search the Arabs for guns and leave us alone," Avraham said.

Another convoy arrived from the opposite direction. A taxi came to a halt parallel to ours. Avraham stuck his head out of the window.

"How was the trip from Jerusalem?" he shouted at the driver.

"All quiet," the man answered.

"Thank God," said Avraham.

The bus in front of us moved forward.

"All quiet," the driver had said. And I was thinking in the stillness of the car that for Yossi Mendelson it also was quiet. Permanently.

He was my best friend. Our mothers were best friends. They grew up together in Germany. They stayed friends in the Promised Land. Yossi's father was a rabbi. Each Passover my parents and I traveled to Jerusalem to participate in the Mendelsons' Seder.

Yossi was an only child, as was I. He was tall, like his father, red-haired and freckle-faced, like his mother. He had twinkling green eyes from some ancestor unknown to me. He loved to tell jokes and to laugh and sing.

One evening Yossi and his father were walking home after prayers at the Western Wall, down the cobblestones in the ancient, narrow streets of the Old City. A single sniper's bullet hit Yossi in the chest. He died the following day.

We heard about it on the news broadcast on Kol Yerushalayim, the Voice of Jerusalem. Two days later my mother and I attended Yossi's funeral. When they lowered him into the hole in the ground, his skull wobbled in the shroud. My mother held my hand tightly. His mother sobbed. His father shed silent tears. I could feel nothing.

Later that day, in the Mendelsons' apartment, sitting in mourning on a wooden stool, as was the custom, Mrs. Mendelson looked at me and then whispered in my mother's ear. On the bus taking us home to Tel Aviv, my mother told me what her friend had said to her:

"Let him have his dream. Let him go to America."

My mother's eyes filled with tears.

It was in the springtime, when the way to Jerusalem was green with budding trees and a rich brown with freshly-plowed fields, both Arab and Jewish. It was then we buried Yossi. Now, in the chill of winter, I was returning to the place where he no longer lived.

The convoy had made its way down the Mountain of Judea into the valley below. A bus and a car, and a bus and a car, perhaps a dozen altogether, followed one another as if holding on to a lifeline. Soon the mountain rose on both sides of the road.

"Not much more to go," said the sandwich lady.

"Don't give us the Evil Eye," said the woman in the other jump seat with a laugh.

The young man with the beard and the skull cap was asleep. The girl next to me was knitting. I closed my eyes and thought of Yossi, that I wouldn't be seeing him ever again.

The crackling sounds of my childhood. Scores of them at once.

I wanted to hide under my bed.

"Get down, everybody!" shouted Avraham. "Ambush!"

My face hit the floor.

The rat-a-tat of a responding machine gun deafened my ears.

Someone leaned over me. A barrage of something sharp rained on my back. On my head. Was I hit?

I saw my parents holding on to each other as they waved goodbye.

I saw Yossi in his grave.

No. It was I.

I felt the car speeding. Voices shouting. Buses rumbling.

"I got hit. My arm." It was Avraham's voice.

"Can you drive?" a woman asked.

"Yes, for now."

Sounds of ripping fabric. A gasp of pain.

Then it was quiet.

"You can get off the floor now," the girl next to me said as she put components of her submachine gun back into the knitting bag. Empty shells were all around me, empty shells that had bounced off my body as their contents zapped through the air.

The second woman in the jump seat was bending forward, bandaging Avraham's arm. A first-aid kit lay next to her on the seat. Avraham grasped the steering wheel with both hands.

"Just a bullet scrape," she said. "You'll be fine."

I caught his eye in the rearview mirror. I must have looked grim. He smiled.

"I'll be okay. Just doing my duty."

So he was in the Haganah detail! As was the girl next to me. The woman administering first aid probably was a Haganah nurse. They risked their lives. And I . . . I was going to America.

I leaned back in my seat thinking of how I'd just been spared. Thinking of my father's warning, not to sit by the door. The bullet that scraped Avraham—it could have struck me!

Suddenly my father's voice echoed in my mind. "Sands, flies, and Arabs."

I thought of Mrs. Mendelson's message to my mother: "Let him have his dream. Let him go to America."

I closed my eyes. What to do?

* * *

The trees and houses on the outskirts of Jerusalem were a welcome sight. The convoy rolled down Jaffa Road, the city's main thoroughfare, to the Central Bus Station. We all shook hands, congratulating each other on having survived. "Shalom. Shalom. Peace be with you."

A man on a stretcher was carried from one of the buses into an ambulance. The only motions were those of the men carrying him. His eyes stared ahead. I felt a needle in my heart. He was probably dead. Did he have a mother? A father? Wife and children? The ambulance door was shut. The vehicle pulled out of the station. The siren was not turned on.

"Now tell me why you're really in Jerusalem," Avraham said, as we stood on the sidewalk outside the station. "Your father wouldn't send you on an errand in times like these."

I looked at him and said nothing.

"You're leaving, aren't you? Your visa's come through."

I nodded. I couldn't lie to him now.

He grabbed my arms.

"If you leave, you have no right to come back," he said. "Because we're all doing our duty. Risking our lives for a common goal. And you're walking away from it. For your own selfish reasons."

He released me. Then he turned back into the bus station where another convoy was assembling. He would be in it, of course.

I sat on a nearby bench, my head in my hands.

America, the Goldene Medine, where dreams come true.

Eighteen years old. To be on my own, in the land of

opportunity, with no father and mother to tell me what to do. To have my whole life ahead of me. Who knew how far I could go in America? And then, some day, I would be back. Yes. Of course. I would be back.

Times Square, Broadway, Hollywood, palatial homes, swimming pools, cars, nice clothes, malt shops, jitterbug, jazz.

No war. No Arabs. No shooting. No bombs.

I hailed a cab to the American consulate. A sudden rainstorm rumbled down from the skies. After a while the cab came to a stop. The driver turned around.

"This is as far as I go," he said. "The consulate is inside the Arab quarter. You don't expect me to drive there, do you?"

"How'll I get there?"

"Walk." The driver laughed.

On that afternoon of December 26, 1947, a visa was stamped into my passport. Arab bullets bounced off the armored car that subsequently took me and other passengers to Lod Airport. I arrived at LaGuardia on January 12, 1948. The Jewish state would be established four months later.

I've visited Israel many times. But I've never seen Avraham.

I've never looked him up.

Wadad Saba

Wadad Saba came to the United States on a scholarship when she was twenty-one years old. Only recently retired from a thirty-five-year career as a professor of music at Seattle Pacific University, she has been very active in teaching voice and opera in the Seattle community. In addition, she has been a frequent vocal soloist and served as musical director in several Christian churches.

Forced to flee Jerusalem in 1948, when she was fifteen, Saba is passionate about the plight of the Palestinian people, which she depicts in her story. She says, "The Palestinians are a disenfranchised people whose country is still subject to the 'iron fist' of occupation by Israel."

A Christian Palestinian's Story

I can assume that only those readers who have lost their home and their country will really understand the trauma I experienced when, two months before my sixteenth birthday, I found myself forced to start life all over again with a new identity in a new residence.

I was born in Jerusalem, Palestine, and lived there for almost sixteen years preceding the creation of the state of Israel in 1948. You see, for centuries there was no country known as Israel. My country was known as the land of Palestine, spoken of so prominently in the Biblical record, and that land clearly belonged to its native inhabitants, the Palestinians. But Palestine was literally stolen from me and my countrymen and re-named Israel in 1948 with the help of the Western world, who felt guilty for allowing the Holocaust against the Jews of Europe and were not eager to have them immigrate to their lands.

I am a Palestinian Arab and proud of it. My parents were Christians and I was raised in the Anglican church of St. Paul's in Jerusalem where my grand-father, the Reverend Salih Saba, had been the rector.

I grew up in a multi-cultural and multi-religious so-ciety. There were people living in Palestine who came from all over the world. My home in the part of West Jerusalem known as the Greek Colony had a high con-centration of Greeks. Within walking distance was the German Colony where I went to kindergarten and first grade in a German school run by Lutherans. Our neighbors and friends were Muslims. My father's best friend and his physician were Palestinian Jews.

Palestine at the time was a British mandate and when World War II threatened to involve the Middle East, the British government shut down my German school, rounded up all my German teachers, friends, and classmates and sent them to undisclosed "deten-tion camps." I never heard from them again!

This was my first experience of loss and disruption in my life. I was seven years old and had no idea how much more was still in store for me. From the age of nine to sixteen, I attended a private Catholic school for girls where some of my friends were Jewish while others were Muslim and Christian. The last two years at St. Joseph's High School, I learned that some of my Jewish classmates were going away on weekends to Zionist kibbutzim for military training which they eventually were to use against me, my family, and my people.

At the age of thirteen, I remember walking to a neighborhood movie house and being shot at by Zionist snipers. One day at school when I was fourteen, we all had to duck under our desks when an Israeli tank drove by the school and sprayed the classrooms of Arab children with gunfire.

I remember spending many nights in terror, afraid that my father and mother would be ambushed by Jewish terrorists on their way home from visiting friends in the neighborhood and cringing each time I saw my dad pick up a loaded gun for self-protection when he left the house.

I remember studying by candlelight many nights to avoid making our home a visible target for terrorist attacks.

I also remember playing the piano at noon on July 22, 1947, and being startled by a horrendous explosion that shook our house. It was the King David Hotel, headquarters of the civilian government of Palestine, that was blown up by the Irgun Zvai Leumi gang, an underground Zionist terrorist organization headed by Menachem Begin who later became Prime Minister of Israel. Two hundred and fifty civilians were killed in that attack, many of them friends of my family. The sense of loss and grief I experienced are indescribable.

I remember the horrific news of the April 10, 1948 massacres of the village of Deir Yassin where 254 Palestinian men, women, and children were raped and slaughtered by the Stern gang with whom Itzak Shamir was involved. He, ironically, also later became Prime Minister of Israel.

This infamous massacre signaled a change in the history of Palestine. It was, by the Israeli leadership's own admission, a deliberate attempt to terrorize the Arab civilian population and drive them out of their homes and towns. With the continuation of such attacks, their plan succeeded. Millions of Palestinians fled their homes in fear, hoping to return when peace was restored. Fifty years later, they are still waiting!

As the situation became more and more intense, my parents decided they would send us children (four girls) to spend a few weeks with our aunt in Cairo, Egypt, and then send for us when things settled down. I left Jerusalem with my three sisters on a bus on May 11, 1948 bound for Cairo, and on May 15th Israel raised its flag, declared itself a state, and closed its borders.

The United States under President Truman recognized Israel as a legitimate country and Palestine simply and suddenly disappeared from the map. Because the borders were shut down, we were unable to return to our home in Jerusalem.

For two years the only news we had about our mother and father were occasional cryptic Red Cross messages. It was 1950 before Mother joined us in Lebanon and 1951 before we were reunited with my father in Beirut.

My father was a successful established businessman in Jerusalem representing Firestone Tires, Diamond Trucks, and automotive spare parts. When Israel declared itself a state, it "requisitioned" all my father's assets as enemy property. This included looting the huge inventory in his store and seizing several shipments still waiting to be unloaded. He told me that even his bank account with Barclays Bank was frozen by the Israeli government. All attempts to recover his losses through the Israeli courts were fruitless. In despair, and knowing that this long separation from his four daughters was unacceptable, he decided to leave Jerusalem and join us in Beirut. In order to do so, he was forced to sign a release saying he would never seek to reenter his homeland and that he would not claim any compensation for his home, his business, or his bank account.

What a price to pay! Father's spirit was broken and he never quite recovered from this ordeal. Still, I consider myself as one of the lucky ones among the millions of displaced Palestinians. My family was able to relocate in Lebanon because of my mother's Lebanese origins, and we were able to find work and gradually get on with our fractured lives. That was not the case for the majority of Palestinians who till this day are living in refugee camps under conditions that make the slums of New York seem like resorts. Or they are eking out an existence on land in the West Bank and Gaza, experiencing the daily inhumanity of military occupation and oppression.

When I first left Palestine, and saw what the Jewish immigrants from Europe were doing to my country and my people, I naturally was filled with anger and hatred. As a teenager, I would have gladly picked up a gun and shot the first Israeli I saw. It took some years before my faith in God was rekindled and my acceptance of the love of God impacted my feelings of hostility, making me realize that hatred is an unproductive emotion. Nevertheless, to this day, my sense of outrage has never left me. It has become more intense the more I learn about the continuing horrors of Israel's occupation of the West Bank and Gaza. I find myself motivated by a heightened sense of justice to work for the end of these horrors. God requires justice, mercy, and righteousness! I believe that as a Christian I must stand up and speak out wherever these values are violated.

As a Palestinian in exile, I was unable to return to my homeland for many years. Finally, with an American passport, I made my first journey back to Jerusalem in 1990, forty-two years after leaving it. I cannot describe the torrent of emotions and reactions that flooded my mind and heart upon seeing my beautiful hometown again. It is such an incredible place—even the air is special! But the heartache I felt when I observed what was going on there was overwhelming. I remembered Jerusalem as a beautiful, quiet city worthy of its name, "the City of Peace." It used to be surrounded by rolling hills, covered with wild flowers, where we as children went to watch the sunrise every Sunday and pick wild anemones and cyclamens. Seeing the city again, ripped apart by pain and tragedy, surrounded by ugly concrete settlements, and teeming with submachine gun–toting Israeli soldiers and civilians, I wept.

While I was there I determined that I would find and visit the home in which I grew up, which I knew was occupied by Jewish settlers. After all those years, I had no trouble remembering exactly where it was located, and I had a friend drive me there. Upon seeing my home, tears welled up in my eyes as my heart thumped at a rate I don't care to experience again.

I had heard of many incidents of Palestinian Americans returning to their occupied homes only to be greeted with stones and insults. I wasn't ready for such an experience.

I noticed that the first floor of the two-story house had been converted into a grocery and flower shop and that someone was living upstairs. I bought a nice bouquet of flowers, hoping it would offset any feeling of hostility or confrontation, and I cautiously climbed the stairs. A tall, handsome, elderly woman answered the door and I began to tell her in English who I was and why I was there.

"Sorry," she said, "only Hebrew! Sarah, come!"

Her thirty-something daughter came to the door and translated what I had to say to her mother, whereupon they invited me in warmly and brought Arabic coffee and cookies as my friend and I sat in the living room—which used to be my bedroom—and engaged in a most incredible dialog.

The mother wanted to know how and why I left my home. I told her in detail about my childhood, the terror of war, the escape to safety, the loss of all our possessions, the three-year separation from my parents who had fled from the house and sought refuge in a Lutheran hospice. All of this was translated into Hebrew by Sarah.

Then I asked Sarah how she and her mother came
to possess my home. She started by saying that her
mother came from Iraq. I turned in amazement and
asked the mother if she spoke Arabic. Yes, of course
she did. All of a sudden the conversation did a round-
about and what I told the mother she translated into
Hebrew for her daughter.

She had come to Jerusalem from Iraq and housed
her family in a small dwelling that she found vacant.
But some days later, an armed soldier ordered her out
at gunpoint since it was a place he wanted for himself.
He promised to find her another home and that home
was mine.

When I got ready to leave, I asked for permission to
take some pictures of the house with its familiar color-
ful Italian tile floor, its old weathered wooden shutters
and its gorgeous white stone structure. Sarah brought
out her camera too and took pictures of me and my
friend with her and her mother. She put her arms
round my shoulders and with a slight tremor in her
voice said, "Isn't it awful what people do to people?
Next time you come to Jerusalem, please come visit
your home again."

Tears were the obvious response for both of us. For
one brief moment, by the grace of God, the walls of
partition dissolved and traditional enemies responded
heart to heart.

Hope of reconciliation, yes! But I was overcome by
sadness as, on my way back from the house, I passed
Israeli soldiers kicking Arab boys, overturning fruit
carts, beating up children to the point of breaking their
bones, forcing Palestinian shopkeepers to close their
shops, and bulldozing and wrecking Arab homes.

* * *

This oppression of my people is still going on today and in many ways it has intensified. I fear it will continue as long as we allow it to do so. People must see each other as people . . . and work together for peace *and* justice. One cannot occur without the other!

Ibtisam S. Barakat

A *Palestinian woman who lived under Israeli occupation in the West Bank until she was twenty-two, Ibtisam Barakat graduated from Birzeit University, went on to get a master's degree in journalism at the University of Missouri, and is now a writer in Columbia, Missouri. She is the author of numerous articles focusing on the needs of young people.*

Although she is far from her homeland, Barakat is involved with the international struggle for human rights and has given a great deal of thought as to how Palestinians and Israelis can achieve the justice necessary for lasting peace. "It is of utmost importance to me," she says, "that I work with others toward a vision of justice and dignity for all, and toward transcending all hurts of racism, oppression of females, and injustices affecting young people."

Marked for Destruction

The war came to us at sundown. My mother had just announced that our lentil-and-rice dinner would be ready as soon as Dad arrived. She picked up my infant sister, held out a plump breast, and began to rock and feed her. I knew I wanted to be the one rocking in my mother's arms.

My two brothers, the noisy inseparables, were chasing one another around my mother's jasmine garden, and I stood at the door awaiting my father's emergence from the evening shadows on the long gravel road that led to our home. Like every evening, I was preparing to run toward him with all the vigor of my three and a half years of life. But because I had only one pair of shoes and was only allowed to wear them on important occasions lest I wear them out, I often hopped my way along the gravel as I swung my eyes between the ground and the shadow of the man I loved.

My dad was my giant ally, and before the war I had an unwavering sense that all was well as long as he came home at the end of the day. Each time I met him, he embraced me with a splendid smile that made his right eye fade into the shape of a crescent moon. He reached out to me with his loofah-like hand, and I half hung in the air as I grasped two of his fingers and walked.

My dad often gave me five tries at guessing what the treat he had in his pocket for me and my two brothers was. When I could not guess by the fifth time, he gave me the first letter of the word, and then I guessed for certain unless it was a new treat he had brought.

But on the evening of June 5th, 1967, my dad was the one who was rushing toward me. He was in an urgent hurry, and I could see his face had no smile. His speed spelled hazard from a distance, and although he was saying something, it was only when he was closer that I could hear his wretched words: "Run back and tell your mother the war has started!" he said. I did not fully comprehend the command, but everything in me sensed the danger in those words.

As I ran home, I fell on the gravel and scraped my knees, but I didn't feel the pain except for a moment. I had sensed that my dad did not need to be bothered by a crying child. Somehow I made myself stop feeling my pain.

My mom seemed to know exactly what dad's words meant. Her shocked response was so frightening that it would forever stick in my mind as the symbol of the gravest lamentation and loss. She struck her face with both her hands and dug her nails into her terror-stricken cheeks. And then she scraped. She said not a word, and her eyes gazed into the distance. I could tell that her soul had momentarily departed the space of our kitchen where we all stood paralyzed.

Many years later, I learned that in those lines mother scraped on her face was the story of a woman whose heart had been torn by war once before. My mother was a child during the war of 1948—the war that took place after Jews self-declared Palestinian land as their national home and named it Israel. When the war started in 1948, my mother was asleep, and in the cruelty of an inexplicable moment, her mother left her behind.

Now, standing in the kitchen as my father's words hung in the air like a brandished sword, my mother was reminded that her family, her people, and everything Palestinian were bound for mass destruction once again.

My dad held my mother's arm tenderly. He spoke to her in the manner he spoke to me about the importance of closing my eyes and falling asleep when he turned off the light at night. He told her that he had heard that the planes had been targeting homes in particular and that the safest thing would be to turn off all the lights, leave our home immediately, and sit in the garden in the trench he had been digging for a water culvert while we decided what to do.

He also said he wanted to listen to the radio to find out which specific areas were being attacked, but the only radio we owned was an enormous, oven-like set that he thought would be unsafe to carry into the trench.

Before we left the house, my mother snatched my infant sister and held on to her tightly. My two brothers and I held on to my mother's dress and we all marched outside.

Inside the trench I glued my body to my brothers' and my heart surrendered to the rhythm of our vigilant breaths, all rising and falling in anxious unison. With the tip of my head, I reached to touch my father's arm that was surrounding us. His other arm enclosed my mother who was attempting to quiet our infant sister whose siren cries threatened to draw fatal attention to our hiding place, and as there was no room for love and lullabies in the tight trench, my mother sharply howled at my sister who quickly abandoned all noise.

My father and mother exchanged a few whispers and then my dad announced that there was no escape for a human from destiny. "What is written on the forehead, the eye must see," he said. Then he prayed for gentleness in what the few coming hours or days held for us.

My dad's pained voice was bitter with the disillu-

sionment of a captured wild bird. My brothers and I
understood that something beyond what we'd ever
learned or would ever understand was about to happen
to our father. We reached for his clothes and held on
to him firmly. I remember feeling that I would do anything at all that would make my father feel happy one
more time.

As darkness came and shut off our senses, I could
neither see my body nor the faces of my father, mother,
and brothers except in memory. Then suddenly my
mother whispered to my father that she could hear
footsteps coming. My father ordered us to freeze. I
stopped myself from breathing.

It quickly became apparent that the footsteps were
those of a string of people from neighboring villages
who were fleeing their homes.

Raising his voice only loud enough that they could
hear him, my father questioned the crowd about the
news.

A man's voice answered. "After their planes attack,
they will be combing the area house by house. The
word is that they will butcher every living thing that
they find."

My parents exchanged a few whispers and then
quickly agreed that it was time for us to join all the
fleeing people. "Death in a group is mercy," my dad
said.

"I want to get into the house and bring out some
food. The children are famished," my mother said.

"But hurry, and don't light even a match," my dad
warned.

My mother tucked our silent sister into his arms,
murmured to us that she would be back in no time,

and disentangled her body from the trench with the vigilance of a leopard prudently moving toward its prey.

Before we could settle into the thought that food was within reach, a violently pulsing noise sliced through our dread. Bullets were being fired at my mom. She let out a shrill scream and then sunk into calm.

My brothers and I screamed but we quickly stopped when my father told us that we were being "targeted" and he commanded us to remain silent and still.

The giant bullets seemed to have originated from a plane that zoomed above our heads and trailed off into the distance. It set monstrous nearby patches of the darkness afire. We could hear the piercing noises everywhere and couldn't tell what side of the sky would be the next to blaze.

After he'd secured our one-year-old sister in our arms, my father stretched his body out to my mother's and grabbed her foot. He pulled her into the center of the trench.

Seeming to have lost awareness of her body, Mother frantically searched herself for a fatal injury as she said, "I want to see my children one last time before I die."

After realizing that Mom had miraculously escaped injury, my dad held her to his chest and reassured her that all was well. "They missed," he whispered. And the warmth in his voice allowed my blood to flow anew through my veins. My mother, shocked by the astounding events, had nothing to say. Then suddenly in a harsh voice she demanded that we immediately leave.

It seemed very unwise, but mother picked up our one-year-old sister and began walking toward the house. My two brothers and I leapt after her as my father prayed hysterically that we come to no harm.

Inside the house my mother snatched the pot of lentil-and-rice from the kitchen and wrapped it in a rag. Then she dashed into the darkness and searched for a bundle of golden bracelets that were her dowry when she married my dad. I could hear her sigh of relief when she found the gold.

Then she commanded that we put on our shoes immediately. But I did not know where my shoes were and the house was entirely consumed in darkness. "I don't know where my shoes are," I muttered.

"Just find them," she said. And I and my two brothers obediently searched until we found our shoes and went outside.

My mother and father were whispering urgently in the dark. My father said that if we didn't die that night, we'd have to sleep in the wilderness. He and my mother agreed that he must get some clothes and blankets to sleep in. When he came out of the house with a mound in his arms, my parents argued whether or not to lock the door. They finally agreed to lock it and take the key with us.

Fleeing people continued to pass by our house, spreading words of impending terror. A breathless man told my father that there were no people left in the village from which he and his group had fled. He also said that they were fleeing to the caves first, and then to Jordan—our neighboring country—which might take a few days to reach.

"What caves?" my dad asked.

"Run with us," the man said before merging into the darkness.

My father announced that we were to move immediately with the crowd for that seemed to be our last chance of being with people and escaping an isolated fate.

My inseparable brothers had already put on their shoes and held each other's hands tightly. My mother had secured my sister between her arms. My father strained to see the road from behind the mound of clothes and blankets in his arms. But I, in spite of all my desperate attempts to comply with my parents' commands, was unable to put my shoes on. They were lace-up shoes that my three-and-a-half-year-old hands were unable to lace in the dark.

"I can't put them on," I cried in a hushed voice, lest I attract attention and we all die. "Help me." But no one answered.

At that moment, a new wave of fleeing people rushed by our door. As they hurriedly disappeared, everything faded into stillness. And my family was gone. I could not grasp that they had walked away with the crowd and left me behind.

I wanted to cry aloud, but my voice had drowned in my dread. Then I could see that the only hope for me was to leave my shoes aside, storm through all that I felt, and run in the direction the fleeing people ran. As I began to move, sounds of distant gunshots, screeching noises unexpectedly swelled and then subsided.

When I looked behind I could no longer see the giant shadow of our home. And the world within and around me seemed to fade into the ghastly unknown.

The gravel grated sharply at my feet. Once again, I

commanded myself not to feel. When my wary ears detected voices, I awaited them cautiously, and when they approached, I attached myself to the end of their caravan. Settling into the rhythm of this rapidly-moving crowd, I could hear men talking about what I understood was a smaller group of their townspeople who had left early and who would await them near the road to the caves.

The mention of the caves filled my heart with a hope that my family would perhaps be with the group we would eventually join. But my hopes were pierced by the flares that lit up the darkness and formed a dome in the sky. People in the caravan began to pray aloud. They said that God is one.

The lights in the sky blinded us and then there was a barrage of bombs. The feeling was that the moment of definitive destruction had arrived. But as the lights and sounds of bombardment continued and no one in my crowd was hit, it became apparent that neighboring areas were the immediate targets of attack.

Our group continued to move on, although all voices had sunk into a solemn calm. As we went, I noticed that we were joining other clusters of people, as ghostly and stunned as we were. Among those ahead of us, I thought I saw my mother holding my sister, her thick, dark braid wagging on her back.

Our group sped up to meet the group in front of us and my numbed feet flew forward. The lights in the sky came and went, but I kept my eyes on my mother's braid. I dashed through the big silent parade to survival. I pushed and threw myself through the hurrying legs of people who cursed in muted voices, lest we all die. And I moved to where I thought I saw my mom.

When I was only a few steps behind the dark braid that now wagged frantically, life meant nothing but reaching a step closer. And when my fingers touched her dress, the war seemed to halt.

Thinking that I was with my mother again, I began to feel the feverish fire in my feet, and I could no longer ignore the pain. I tightened my grip on her dress. I let myself weep a little and let her dear dress take my weight. That respite lasted only a few seconds however. As new war flares blinked and widened their predator eyes, a disturbed face turned to scold me.

"Who are you?" she asked as she sternly shook her dress free from my hand. I could see that the woman was not my mother.

I dropped my hands to my sides, gripped my own dress, and could feel neither terror nor pain. My eyes searched for no one, and it mattered not whether I walked alone or had others around.

When we approached the caves, voices deliberated as to whether we should hide in them or continue to walk. A few of the people settled for the caves, but I found myself walking with those who chose to continue on the road.

As we arrived at a road, dawn lit up the world and announced yet another day of war. I could see more people around me than I'd ever seen before. They were gazing into the horizon where a long line of unanswered prayers hung from the sky. They were cursing. They were struggling to swallow the bitter news. They were begging one another for a drink of water. And some were still praying. And all awaited a miracle to transport us away from the war, away from our home.

I wandered among the faces and somehow saw my

father, my mother, and my two brothers. I could neither cry nor smile. And although I walked up to them,
and they to me, we had become a heartful of fright
estranged.

My family and I arrived in Jordan. We awaited a
chance to return, and that came to us under the protection of the International Red Cross. After four
months and thirteen days, there was a narrow window
of opportunity for us to make up our minds about
staying in Jordan or returning home. Many families
worried that they might be harmed if they went back,
and when the window closed quickly they remained
permanently outside. But our family was among the
first to return.

My mother insisted, "If they live, I want my children
to know who they are!"

Upon our return home, there were soldiers everywhere. They marched with their guns in long lines on
the gravel road leading to our home. My brothers and
I stopped playing outside for a long time.

And over the years I understood that the war was
only the start, and that our lives, and all things Palestinian, were marked for destruction by a fire that
would not be put out.

Marina N. Riadi

Marina Riadi's family lived in Jerusalem until they were forced out in May 1948. Now living in Atlanta, Georgia, she has worked for peace organizations in the Middle East, Europe, and the United States for twenty-five years and has had several books and articles published about the Palestinian-Israeli peace process.

In this poignant story of her twelve-year-old yearning to understand the children and the adults caught up in the Israeli-Palestinian conflict, one can see the roots of Riadi's lifelong interest in peace work.

Born in Bethlehem

My first experience of the war in 1967 brought many questions to my young mind, some of which still are unanswered. I was twelve years old and very eager to know how Israeli children my age felt during the war. Were they as frightened as I was? Did they worry that they might lose their parents or other family members as I did?

Naturally, after the Israeli army occupied our little town of Bethlehem and the rest of our lands on the

West Bank and the Gaza Strip, we were not allowed to travel freely within those lands. We were not allowed into Israel proper either. We became captives in our own homes, forced to stay in our small towns. I wanted so much to travel into Israel and see the Israeli people, their families, and their children.

On some gray and lonesome summer afternoons, when Bethlehem became very quiet, I would gaze at the horizon and the yonder hills and imagine what it would be like to cross the "borders," thereafter known as the "Green Line," and discover how children lived in Israel. I wanted to find out about their lives, their hopes, their fears, and their dreams.

My father, observing the extent of my curiosity, decided to take me on a short venture into Israel. My mother and the rest of our family became very anxious as my father announced that he and I were going to West Jerusalem to explore and talk to Israelis.

My mother gasped and with half a breath said, "You'll be arrested for going into Israel without a permit. Then what will I do? Where will I find you? Plus, you're taking the child with you, which makes two of you to worry about. No, you're not going!"

But, my father, being as determined and stubborn as always, decided not to heed my mother's warnings, and off we went to Jerusalem.

I will never forget the elation and excitement that I experienced as soon as we got into the taxi that drove us to the border beyond which we would have to walk. Neither my father nor I thought about how long the walk would be. We were both ready to go and full of the energy and stamina needed for such a venture. I walked up Jaffa Road, then Ben Yehuda Street, and over to King George Street. I observed and scrutinized every passerby, while trying to keep a low profile and blend in with the rest of the pedestrians.

My father was cautious not to attract any particular attention, but at the same time he was totally relaxed and confided that we were going to be perfectly safe and undisturbed. He was right. The more we walked and looked in store windows to check out Israeli merchandise and compare it to what we had in our Bethlehem stores, the more I felt relaxed and happy to be walking along with my father in a city which he loved dearly and to which he belonged until he was forced out in 1948.

I felt so proud to see that my father knew his way around West Jerusalem and could show me the new construction that had taken place since he had last seen it. Occasionally he would wonder about the location of a certain cafe or a restaurant where he and his friends had met. So, we would stop by at one of the stores and he would ask the owner about the place. Most of the time we found out that the store owners were new Jewish immigrants who did not know the sites or the city as well as my father. I felt very proud to realize that my father, who had not lived in West Jerusalem for the past twenty years, knew the city better than its present inhabitants.

But this fact brought a dilemma to my mind. I started wondering about how someone like my father can know a city which is not his anymore better than those who now live in it. Why did he have to leave it if he knew it and loved it so dearly? What were the circumstances that extracted him so abruptly from his roots? Did he have to go in order for the new immigrants to come. And, if so, why? Why couldn't he stay while the new immigrants came in and settled? He could have helped them get acquainted, oriented them to Jerusalem, and given them his knowledge and love for the city.

All these questions were racing in my mind as we crossed from one street to another. Occasionally I would look up at my father to see how he was feeling and if he still had the strength for more exploration. But, having been the strong athlete that he had been for years, my father was tireless and gathered more vigor as we walked on.

We arrived at the YMCA. He pointed out its high tower to me and described how he used to go there directly after school to work out, play racket ball, and practice boxing. He also showed me the local radio broadcast station where he played his music and performed on the air. He told me how on many occasions he would play along with Jewish musicians who were new immigrants from Europe—mostly from Germany and Poland. He told me how much he enjoyed learning from them about European musical instruments and teaching them about Middle Eastern instruments. I watched him yearn for those days and for those people with whom he developed strong friendships.

I watched him become sad and disillusioned as he described his life prior to 1948. He spoke fondly of his Jewish friends and even told me of a Jewish family whose daughter he used to take out. He said that her mother often told him that she prayed fervently that her daughter and my father would one day marry each other.

I listened carefully to his stories, absorbed every

event and minute detail, as if it were an important milestone in the journey of my own life. I sensed my father's pain as he described the separation and the forced parting from his home, his city, his friends, and—most of all—his fond memories.

I was getting a little hungry, even though my mother had fed us a good and substantial lunch, in case we did not make it back home in time for the next meal. My father suggested we go for a snack of coffee and cake and chose the Kapulski pastry shop, a small cafe which was in business in 1948 and was one of the few that continued to operate. We walked in and, once more to my amazement, my father seemed familiar with the family who owned the place. He inquired about the welfare of the owners he had known, but, to his disappointment, he was told that even though the present owners were familiar with the names of the past owners, the place had been sold to new owners who decided to keep the old name.

We sat down, had a beverage and a pastry, and observed passersby and walk-ins. My father told me that Kapulski was the best pastry shop in West Jerusalem and that his family would order platters from there for parties, receptions, birthdays, and other social events. It was another landmark of my father's years in Jerusalem.

Eventually we both realized that we were getting tired. In addition, the emotional and sentimental feelings that surfaced with all the recollections of Jerusalem started to weigh on us, with the heavier burden laying on my father's shoulders.

On our way back towards the border, I stopped to look in the window of a music store. I loved music and

I bought and collected all the latest hits and musicals from movies as soon as they were available in the market. My eye caught the album of the movie *The Sound of Music*. I was astonished to see that the album had arrived and was available for sale. I gasped and looked up at my father. Without saying a word, he understood what I wanted. He looked at me and said, "Alas! I'm out of Israeli money. This has to wait for the next time we come up here."

Upon hearing that, I was so disappointed that I was at the point of crying over the album. One more look at me and my father decided to walk into the store. I lingered behind, a little apprehensive of what my father was up to. This was only a few days after the 1967 war, Israeli currency had not gotten distributed in our markets, and our Jordanian currency was no longer good in Israeli markets. Moreover, I was well aware that my father and I needed to remain incognito on our venture lest we end up being stopped, asked for a permit, and arrested for going into Israel.

But my father was fearless as usual. He walked up to the music store owner and, stretching out his hand to greet him, introduced himself to the Israeli man. I was still standing halfway between the entrance to the store and my father. The store owner responded in a friendly, welcoming manner to my father's greeting and shook hands with him. I was bewildered. I asked myself if my father knew that man before 1948. Was he a friend, a neighbor, an acquaintance? I thought my father and I had agreed not to bring any attention to ourselves—not to reveal our identity—and especially not to tell anyone where we were from.

I started wondering if my father was making a big

mistake and one that would jeopardize our safety. But, at the same time, I knew my father very well and believed strongly in his good judgment and common sense. I decided to let go of all fears and give my full attention to the situation as it developed. I also knew deep down in my heart that my father would only do the right thing and that we were safe.

The next thing I heard was my father asking the store owner if he would accept Jordanian currency. The man responded that not only would he accept Jordanian currency, but that he would also honor it. I became completely confused. I thought we were enemies meeting in the aftermath of the war, and now we were about to make a commercial transaction with Jordanian currency in an Israeli store where the owner is paying homage to Jordanian money. I started doubting my own capacity for understanding reality.

The music store owner proceeded to explain to us that he was a new immigrant from Iraq and that he, himself, was new to Jerusalem. In fact, as soon as he spoke to us in Arabic I could hear a different accent and dialect from ours.

My father divulged our tightly held secret and told him that he was from Jerusalem and that he grew up in the vicinity. He also explained to him that we were now living in Bethlehem and he was bringing me to visit his city and share with me his past history and memories. I could tell the man was moved. With tearful and very expressive and compassionate eyes, he looked at my father indicating that he fully understood the tragedy.

I, still a spectator watching every move and interaction between the two men, was still worried about our safety and return home. I was also getting anxious and wondered if and when the transaction would take place so that I could take my album and run home to listen to it.

When all was said about the two men's lives and histories—the Israeli man's experience in Iraq and my father's life in Jerusalem—my father explained the reason for our going into his store. The man seemed to understand my father's wish to please me and buy me the album with Jordanian money. He said that he, himself, had children and knew what it meant when a child wanted something.

I wished I could meet his children, especially those who were close to my age. I wanted to ask them about the war and what happened to them. I wanted to find out about their experience as victors and winners of that war. I simply wanted to know them.

The music store owner walked over to one of the shelves behind the counter, pulled out a brand new album, put it in a paper bag, and handed it over to me. I was delighted and ready to go before anyone else, who might be less friendly and understanding, discovered who we were. My father handed the man the Jordanian money, but, to my amazement, the man would not take it. Instead, he told my father that we could pay him the next time we came to Jerusalem. He said that because of the exchange rate the album would cost my father much more if he paid in Jordanian money rather than in Israeli money.

My father did not care the least about the price and insisted that he take the money, placing it in his hand. The man took the money and handed it over to me saying, "You have a wonderful father. I hope you know that. There aren't many people in this world as honest and straightforward as your father. Do appreciate him and learn all you can from him."

I was in total agreement with what he said, for I already knew the value of my father. I was very surprised to see that the man had come to know and value my father as well as I did in such a short time. He insisted on not taking the money and waiting for us to come back on another occasion. My father felt obliged to leave him our name, address, and phone number. But the man refused to take that information, assuring my father that there was no need for that since he was sure we would come back to pay him with Israeli money.

I was totally amazed. I could not understand how that store owner came to know and understand my father in the first place, much less trust us to walk out with his merchandise and go to an area which he could not access easily and safely because of the state of war.

At that point I thought I had to rise to the occasion and prove worthy of such a father. So I offered with some regret to give back the album that I was holding in my hand, close to my heart, and to buy it on our next trip to Jerusalem. I put the album on the counter and sadly walked back toward the door of the store.

The Israeli man followed me with the album and put it in my hand saying, "You see, I want you to come back, I want to see you again." Looking at my father he added, "I hope next time you come you will bring the rest of your family. I would love to meet them all."

I looked up at him and said, "Sir, I'm just curious, how would you know people whom you can trust from those whom you cannot trust?"

He answered without hesitation. "You look at them straight in the eye and you can easily tell those you can trust from those you cannot. Your father, young lady, is beyond all doubt. One look in his eyes, and I could tell that he was a trustworthy man. You are very lucky to have him."

I held the album even closer to my heart, and my father and I thanked him and reassured him that we would be back to pay him in Israeli money as soon as we could.

Victoria Kay-Feinerman

A writer, wife, and mother, Victoria Kay-Feinerman is earning her master's degree in literature at Bar-Ilan University in Ramat Gan. Several of her poems have been published in the university's literary magazine and she has also had her work published in ARC 11, the journal of the Israel Association of Writers in English.

Born in Manhattan, Kansas, Kay-Feinerman didn't live full-time in Israel until she was thirteen. One of very few Jews in Kansas, and one who considered herself religious, she felt isolated until her family moved to Israel. "I was always the Jew, the outsider," she says, "and I knew I belonged with my people."

Now a permanent resident of what she calls her homeland, Kay-Feinerman says she fears for the future of her country: "One of the reasons I decided to have a baby in the middle of my studies is that I was worried what might happen if war broke out and my husband was called to duty. I figured that I'd at least have something left of him in the case that, G-d forbid . . ."

The Yiddish alti zachen, "old things," that echoes throughout this story is a moving counterpoint to the new life Victoria Kay-Feinerman protected within her body just as she protected herself within a sealed room during the Gulf War.

Alti Zachen

"**A**lti zachen, alti zachen!" old things, old things. The tinny-sounding Yiddish phrase is barked over a megaphone propped in the passenger side window of a faded old yellow truck which rolls slowly down the street in the afternoon heat. My nap-time repose disturbed, I get up off the bed and open the window onto the street. A rush of steamy stickiness invades my air-conditioned flat as I look at the ragged orange couch, scratched wooden chairs, small crib, and battered gray refrigerator piled in the back of the truck. The driver would buy or sell.

"*Alti zachen, alti zachen!*"

The dry Arabic accent gives the cry a funny ring, one that never ceases to amaze me. Who would have thought it? An Arab speaking Yiddish! Even I, a Jew, don't know Yiddish. The German-Jewish language is a dead one, killed in the Holocaust, a language which universities must tempt students to learn with the offer of a five-hundred-dollar reward for receiving a decent mark in the course. So why should Arabs, of all people, wish to revive it?

"*Alti zachen, alti zachen!*"

The wail rises and falls. I remember wondering at the start of the Gulf War whether the "*alti zachen*" trucks would continue to sell their wares while the Jews huddled in attics, or whether they would stay shamefacedly at home, reluctant to see the persecution of the original Yiddish speakers—the Yids, the Jews—by their Iraqi cousins. I was seventeen at the time, and I thought that the Arab peddlers' use of the Holocaust language was a touching and sensitive attempt at communication. They felt for us, and I knew that we and they were unified by the fear and hatred of the common enemy of the time. They probably stayed at home rather than drive their trucks around so as to be close to their own sealed rooms when a siren went off, warning of the approach of a Scud missile.

I'll never forget the night the first siren went off! The sharp wailing rose and fell repeatedly, and I groggily opened my eyes. . . . Realization struck, and my heart rose with the siren and stayed high in my throat. The door of my room flew open, and my Dad tersely ushered me upstairs to the sealed room where my mother and two sisters were hurriedly opening their gas mask kits and pulling on coats and pants.

The windows of my parents' room were covered with shiny brown masking tape and large sheets of plastic. The plastic protected us against possible biological or chemical warfare, and the tape kept the windows from shattering. My dad shoved a wet towel under the door and was starting to cover the cracks with tape when we heard someone rapping on the other side. It was the cat. He somehow knew. After a short argument with my mom, my father quickly reopened the door while turning his face from the incoming air. The large white cat dashed under the bed, and the door was sealed. We would watch him to see if the air was clean.

The thick rubber gas mask covered my face and stuck there. It was a steam room inside the mask, and as the eye-windows began to fog up, I began to panic.

I couldn't see, I couldn't breathe, and I wanted out. I could hear the distant booms over the soothing words of the radio announcer and my constant Darth Vader–like breathing. What if they had sent poisonous gas? If I took my mask off to clean the lenses, would I be gassed to death like my great-grandparents in Auschwitz? I lay somewhere in the gray fog world, my hands and feet covered in plastic bags, gasping—gassssping.

We spent many other nights silently crouching upstairs in the sealed room, eventually moving into the closet for further safety, all five of us crushed into the hot little coffin, and I felt like Anne Frank. The cat continued to rush upstairs at the sound of a siren, even after we followed the radio announcer's latest advice and made the basement bomb shelter our sealed room. The cat remembered that the siren meant he must run upstairs and was unable to learn a new meaning for it. As we could not risk our own lives to drag him out from under the third-floor bed, clawing and hissing in sheer wide-eyed fear, we gave in to his inevitable death.

One Friday night, a missile hit too close to my city, Petach Tikva. The lights went out, and the house shook, and the windows rattled. I looked at my parents, wanting to see their expressions. Were we going to die? But the masks confined us each to our separate universe. Like astronauts floating in space, there was a gaping vacuum between us, and I started to pray, "Hear, oh, Israel, the Lord is God, the Lord is One."

The next morning I went for a walk downtown with my gas mask slung in its box over my shoulder. The results of the Kristallnacht crunched under my Sabbath shoes and glittered sharply in the window panes.

Apartment owners peered furtively out of open living rooms at the shattered plastic shutters that littered the streets. *Alti zachen*. Old things.

I look outside my window and watch a neighbor buy a worn yellow lampshade from the Arab dealer of old things.

It was only later that I heard rumor of what the *"alti zachen"* people had done during the missile attacks. They had danced on their rooftops, fiddling and cheering the Scuds on. Probably laughing in Yiddish.

I think of buying a used crib from the *"alti zachen"* man, but the outdoor heat clings to my face in a sweaty mask, and I close the window.

"Alti zachen, alti zachen!"

The truck drives slowly off, and the voice fades away. Perhaps I'll take the course in Yiddish next year. Would it revive the bones of my great-grandparents to do so?

I lay back down on the bed and breathe deeply of the cool air, one hand resting on my ripened belly, the other on the large white cat.

Ghareeb
(Pseudonym)

Seventeen years old when he wrote his story, Ghareeb says, "I am just a young person who wants to live his life without fear . . . [but] I fail to see any feasible solution or hope for peace." A resident of Ramallah, Ghareeb has been witness to too much brutality to have retained his childhood innocence. In his own words: "In my mind the sound of a bullet, the echo of a kick, the cries of the people, and the images of the dead will never be buried." Nevertheless, Ghareeb says that he is "lucky to be alive and out of prison."

A Look into Memory

Most people mark the beginning of their lives by a birthday, wedding, or some other happy event. This forms a launching point after which they remember most of the things that happen in their lives and feel that they are beginning to grow up.

I have marked the end of my childhood with blood. My earliest memories start on December 9th, 1987. I will never forget how everything was closed down, angry soldiers were yelling everywhere, and the TV showed images of lots of dead bodies. The Intifada [Palestinian uprising]—that was the start of my grown-up life.

Schools were shut down right after the uprising started. Teaching was illegal, and to be in school was a crime. Teachers resorted to teaching illegally in their homes. If I had been caught going to my teachers' houses by the Israeli army, I would have been guilty of a crime. At that time, you would spend the night in the worst jail in the area, get beat up, and have to pay a fine.

In the summer of 1988, the schools were reopened. I will never forget one hot August day. My Mom woke me and my brother up for school. We got dressed and were about to eat our breakfast. Suddenly, I heard the sounds of Quran reading coming from all the mosques. I was scared to death.

On our way to school every mosque was lit and the Quran was being read—something that is only done when a major bad thing has happened. When I reached my school, I learned the horrible news: a ninth grade student from the school had been found dead in the mountains outside the city. He had been beaten and tortured and shot to death by the Israeli army, and then he was left for two days. I will never forget the picture of his bloody, swollen corpse.

My next clash with the Israeli army came in the summer of 1990. My brother and I were practicing karate at a local karate club which was right beside an Israeli army post. Stones were thrown at the army and in they came, pouring into the club. They rounded us all up and lined us up against the wall. They separated the older students from the younger students and began practicing their karate kicks on the older students. I stood there in horror as they beat the students up. Then they interrogated us about our names, where we lived, and the whereabouts of our coach.

The Israeli soldiers took the older students down the street and locked us younger students up in the club. They left us there for more than half an hour while we listened to the sounds of their beating the older students. Later they came and told us to "Get out right now!" An eleven-year-old and a thirteen-year-old—my brother and I—hurried away from this place of horror, but the looks on the older students' faces and the sounds of the beatings will echo in my memory forever.

In my mind the sound of a bullet, the echo of a kick, the cries of the people, and the images of the dead will never be buried. I'm carrying a deep wound, a wound that keeps getting deeper and deeper every time peace is postponed and manipulated.

The echoes, the ghosts, and the voices make me wonder: will I ever be able to forgive and forget? Will time ever bury such a tragedy and help me to start over again as a normal human being?

I have lost the innocence in my childhood to the guns and the boots and the sirens. Yet I am lucky, for I have not lost a member of my family to the dungeon or the gun. But I can't help but wonder about my Palestinian brothers who have lost someone—or who are lost themselves. I can't help but wonder, will it ever end?

Redrose
(Pseudonym)

*R*edrose *was eighteen when she wrote this story about student reaction at her secondary school to the Dizengof Square bombing, October 20, 1994. One of her main concerns was to be certain to thank her friend Nir, who typed the manuscript for her. "It's hard to find a friend who charges only my happiness for his time and efforts," she said.*

Sylvia Asher, one of Redrose's teachers at the secondary school she attends in Tel Aviv, informed her about the opportunity for publication in this book and has supported her efforts throughout the lengthy editorial process. Now Redrose, known as "the genius writer" on her school's World Wide Web homepage, is already inquiring about positions in international journalism and is hereby putting out the word that she's looking for a paper in need of an Israeli correspondent.

Although she finds herself giving up in frustration about the Israeli/Palestinian situation at times, Redrose says that "even a lost cause like peace with the Arabs is worth a fight." To illustrate her point, she wants to pass on a metaphor that she learned from her chemistry teacher:

"Two frogs got trapped in a jar of cream. They couldn't jump out of the liquid and they couldn't climb because the sides of the jar were slippery. One frog said, 'By dawn I'll be dead,' and went to sleep. The second frog swam all

night long and in the morning found herself floating on a pat of butter."

Face of Peace

The news will always have new things to report about: calamities, corruption, politics, crime. But here in Israel, in the last three years, calamities came much too often and they were much too sad.

Three years ago that was all it was for us—news. The assassins were killing people every day, but it was so far from us, a minor phenomenon. The uprising was something I heard about in the news—it was a concept, not a reality. Peace? Peace was a lovely word, in fact it was a fashion. If you were against the peace process, it meant you were not enlightened. I imagined that there would be hugs in the streets, harmony, and love. On the 13th of September, 1993, the first peace agreement was signed in Oslo, but for us it was still just news.

But we talked about it every day. Did I say "talked"? Shouted was more like it. You could have seen fireworks when we argued, it was such a loaded issue and everybody was so violently supportive of their own opinion. By the ninth grade those arguments came so often that just the word "Peace" became a match that could light a fire. Where else in the world would you find fourteen-year-olds so interested in politics? Here everybody is interested because here it's not a matter of which candidates' smile is more photogenic; it's a matter of life and death.

Three years ago we felt safe, and as much as the issue was close to our hearts, it scarcely really touched us. Alas, this safe period in our lives came to an end. On the 20th of October, 1994, came fear and terror. We were in class, it was the ten o'clock break, and I was confronting a math exercise that was beyond my concentration.

"Damn! I will never get this right!" I thumped the miserable table that served as a scapegoat for my frustration.

"Are you out of your mind? You scared me to death!" Rinat jumped at me.

"Sorry, this thing is scaring me to death. I will never get it right—not before tomorrow's test anyway."

A shout from the back of the class interrupted our conversation. Lilach, Keren, and Ifat were listening to a radio.

"This isn't happening! It's not real!" Ifat said with amazement.

Then I saw a tear in Ifat's eye and Keren and Lilach looked worried.

"What's wrong?" I asked. And Rinat and I went to listen to the radio.

". . . The number of dead or injured is yet unknown. The chief of police estimates there are between ten to fifteen dead and over fifty injured. We turn this transmission over to our man in the field . . ."

We didn't know at first what this was all about, but it seemed like the world had gone suddenly darker.

"Was there an accident or something?" Rinat asked.

The radio kept on: "The police have sealed this area." (The reporter's voice was trembling.) "So I'm not exactly sure where the explosion took place."

"Explosion! What is he talking about?" Rinat asked.

"I'm standing now at the Dizengof Square—"

My heart ached and I could not believe it.

"—next to the fountain of water and fire . . . The fire of the explosion has faded away, now is the turn of the tears to fall. The situation is not clear now, but I can tell you, you wouldn't want to be where I'm standing."

He was silent for long seconds. "There is blood everywhere. It's horrible! You can see fingers on the floor, and hair covered with blood, and human flesh all over the sidewalk and the road. The bus is split in two. I guess the explosives were at the center of the bus. The chief of police will have a statement within the hour. Until then I return the transmission to the studio. It's a sad day."

Keren turned the radio off. We were stunned and speechless.

A bunch of guys entered the class, back from the break rambunctious and cheerful. Yonni was chasing Yaniv, throwing chalk at him.

Alon entered the class and came toward us. "Did somebody die, or did the math teacher add more material to the test?"

"There has been an assassination at Dizengof," Keren said.

"Dizengof?!" Alon was aghast.

I panicked. "And if it happened in Dizengof, no-where is safe anymore. Allenby is not safe, the central station is not safe! Oh, my God, how will I get to work?"

"Can't you see that is exactly what they were aiming

for—your fear?" Keren cried. "They just want to intimidate you."

"Well, they are doing a fine job intimidating me," Liron said. "And what daunts me even more is that I don't have a clue who 'they' are. It's a faceless, hateful enemy we have. There is no way to fight him."

"Liron, why do you think they picked Dizengof?" Lilach asked rhetorically. "Because for us it's a symbol of routine. Bus 5, which everybody knows. They want to take away our security. They don't care how many people died today. They are just happy they managed to get to Dizengof, to bus 5, the heart of our city. It's a psychological war."

"They are still blowing people away, no matter what their purpose," Liron said.

The history teacher came into the class. Even before she spoke, we could all see on her face that she had heard the news. We loved her lessons. She made history relevant and interesting. We admired her as a human being. She was funny and witty and such a strong woman. I wanted to see her reaction. And even if I forget her exact words, I shall never forget the spirit of those words:

"It's harder for me to teach than it is for you to study. But terror is the lowest point of no return and they have passed it. You have here a live example of what history is all about. 'Blood is the oil of the wheels of history.' When I was teaching you about the horrible losses of the pogroms, the numbers seemed meaningless. You weren't shocked to hear about hundreds of Jews dead at random, out of the blue. Dead because of politics and antisemitism.

"You were shocked about the figures of the Holocaust. SIX MILLION. That's quite a figure. Compared to that, the pogroms were nothing, minor. It didn't look real to you—just something that happened a long time ago.

"Now you have a live example of what the pogroms were all about—an unfair slaughter of people in their own street. It's not a war; you face a faceless enemy, a nameless enemy, an enemy whose only aim is to intimidate, to horrify, to thrust his ways upon us violently. And what are his ways? The same as always, everywhere—'We don't want you here. This land is ours.' But this land is ours and nobody will take our promised land. We've fought for this home because we were homeless. But now we have to stick to our fight more than ever.

"I'm not saying fight the Arabs; I'm saying fight the terror. Terror does not equal Arabs. And I'm not saying fight their terror. I'm saying don't be influenced by it. It's frustrating to punch the air, and you might want to have a scapegoat to hate and to hit, but when your enemy is shapeless, don't shape him into what he isn't.

"I've already seen a new graffiti outside near the gate. Can anybody guess what it said?"

"Death to the Arabs," Liron said.

"If this was a test, it would be the first one you would pass," Alon said cynically.

"No," Liron said. "I've forgotten a word. 'Death to the Arabs and to the Alons.'"

"Sure, why not?" Alon scoffed. "Spray them all like cockroaches! Throw them to the sea with weights. Get real, Liron! You think the world wouldn't notice. Six million Arabs just take a walk and drown."

"What could the world care?" Liron defended her

stand. "The world didn't interfere when six million Jews were slaughtered."

"But the world did interfere, or else you wouldn't be here," Alon said.

"OK, so we'll kill 'em and the world will interfere and say, 'naughty, naughty, don't do it again.' We'll say we're sorry and send our condolences to seven Arab states, along with large checks, and in a few years everything will be forgotten and forgiven and we won't have Arabs anymore."

Liron seemed to have it all figured out. But she was right. That was the nature of the world—to forget horrors, to forgive horror makers.

"I hereby declare you Liron Adolf Hitler," Adi said.

"It's craziness, what you're saying," I said.

"Yes, well, the world is a crazy place. I'm just adjusting," Liron said, waving her hands as if to say "nothing can be done about it."

"No, I mean even your thoughts are non-human. How can you talk about murder as if you were talking of . . . of cockroaches. Haven't you any sympathy for the Arabs' condition? They are like us in the Holocaust. Germany and Poland had been our homeland. And we didn't have any place to go. We expected to be left as we were, but they hated us just as you hate the Arabs now, Liron. And they talked about killing us just as you are talking now. They are no different from what we were back then."

"Oh, yes, they are, honey!" Liron interrupted me. "We didn't throw any stones or blow up any buses. Besides, we didn't have any place to go; they have seven countries. They practically own the whole Mediterranean coast. So, save the 'poor victims of politics' theory for another sucker."

She was harsh. I hadn't the words or the enthusiasm to argue with her.

"Your hatred is plugging your ears to what is right."

"And your innocence is plugging this country from salvation."

"Now, can I continue?" the teacher asked.

"Sure, go ahead," Liron answered shamelessly, and the lesson went on amidst the continuous struggle of opinions.

That evening everybody plugged themselves into their TV sets. Some went to Dizengof to see the horrors with their own eyes, to sympathize with the pain. Radical mobs demonstrated, blaming the whole world—the Arabs, Yitzhak Rabin, Arafat, the left wing—and wishing death to them all. Twenty-two people died that day, but hatred demanded more deaths.

There was so much anger, so much pain, so much candlelight . . . so little hope.

The next bomb was Bet Lead on the twenty-first of January. The same sad story, the same anger and hatred, doubled and tripled as the number of the dead rose in the news. And me, I was just fearing things to come, very confused, but still trying to think positively—naively??

Racheli Tal

Racheli Tal was born in Seattle, Washington, in 1982. When she was five, she and her family emigrated to Israel, where they eventually came to live in the religious settlement called Beit-El.

In the story that follows, written when she was fourteen, Tal gives us an eyewitness account of how deadly the Arab-Israeli conflict can be. In keeping with the Israeli settler goals that she describes, Racheli says that when she grows up she wants to establish a new settlement in the Golan Heights.

My Life on the Firing Line

I was standing on top of the mountain looking down at the valley below. Men with guns and torches were climbing up the mountain. I tried to run away but they had me surrounded. I could see the deep hatred in their black eyes. One of them tried to catch me. I screamed, and then . . . I woke up.

I sat up in bed, sweaty and frightened, but happy to find myself safe at home. If I believed in bad omens I would have taken this as a bad sign, but I had no idea of what was going to happen.

My name is Racheli Tal. I'm fourteen and I live in the Judean religious settlement named Beit-El. I have two parents, Israel and Chana, and two younger sisters, Miriam, aged eleven, and Rikki, who just turned six. Our settlement is nineteen years old and has about eight hundred families. The settlement is very developed, with schools for children up through high school (there are separate schools for boys and girls), a post-high school yeshiva for religious studies for boys, a clothing store, a bakery, an electronics factory, and even a swimming pool.

When I was five and a half years old I came from the U.S. with my parents. We lived for a year in an absorption center and three years in Jerusalem before we moved to Beit-El. I love Beit-El because it's small and I know almost everybody, but sometimes it can be scary. When we ride the bus to Jerusalem we have to go through the Arab city of Ramallah. Sometimes the Arabs throw rocks at us; that's why we aren't allowed to open the windows in any bus or car. The windows are made out of a very strong kind of plastic-glass to keep the rocks from breaking them, but they aren't bulletproof, so if your car gets shot at it can be very dangerous.

I always thought it was kind of odd that it's our state and the Arabs are allowed to hurt us. Today I know things aren't so simple. The Arabs claim the state is theirs because, when the Jews were in exile from the Land of Israel, the Moslems were in control for a few hundred years. They are commanded to do "jihad"—

holy war—against nonbelievers like Jews and Christians. On the other hand, it says ninety-seven times in the Bible that God gave the Holy Land to the Jews and later King David made Jerusalem Israel's capital. That's what all the fighting is about, and that's one of the reasons everything happened last summer.

I remember the day well. Outside the hot sun was blazing. I was sitting in the rec room by the fan, bored out of my mind and trying to think of something to do. I was just about to give up when I heard a knock on the door. "Come in," I shouted.

It was my best friend Naamah. Just then I noticed a huge smile on her face. I could tell she had some news and she was dying to tell me. "All right, spit it out!" I told her.

"Listen, Racheli, you won't believe this. You know the Artis, the mountain that's beyond the swimming pool? The whole settlement is going up there to build a new neighborhood, but the government doesn't know about it."

"Just a minute," I stopped her. "What exactly are we going to do up there? And how do you know all this?"

"We are going to start making foundations for the houses and, until caravans [trailers] are brought, people who volunteer will sleep up there in tents. The chairman of the settlement's governing council called my mother and asked her to be responsible for passing out the message. When my mother told me about it I immediately ran over here. Come on, let's go tell everybody."

But there was no need. Everybody knew about it

already. That's the way it is when you live in a small place.

We started heading up the mountain. It was already four o'clock in the afternoon and it was starting to cool down so the climb wasn't too hard. The mountain is about 3,000 feet high, and from the top you can see the Jewish settlement Ofra and the Arab village Dura el-Kara. They are pretty close to Beit-El.

When we got to the top of the mountain, what we saw was total chaos. The men were putting up tents and tying wires with light bulbs to the generators. The kids and teenagers were clearing away the rocks and thorn bushes. Little kids were running around everywhere and their mothers were just standing watching. Some people were walking around with video cameras. I saw some of my friends moving rocks and making a path, so I went and helped them. I worked for about two hours. I got dirty and scratched by thorns, but I felt good. I knew how the first settlers felt when they came back to Israel after 2,000 years of exile and had to rebuild their land. I felt like I was building my land for something I believed in: the Jews living in Israel, planting and settling it.

That's when my friend Reut tapped me on the back and woke me up from my daydreaming. "Racheli, we're planning to sleep here tonight. Let's go home and ask our parents for permission. I'll meet you by the swimming pool in an hour."

"Great, let's go," I said, and we headed down the mountain.

It wasn't easy to persuade my parents to allow me to sleep on the mountain. Since Yitzhak Rabin came to power, the settlements have not been allowed to build

houses, so what we were doing was illegal and the police and army might come and try to take us down
forcefully. Similar things were happening in another
settlement named Efrat, and the army came and violently pulled them off their mountain. My parents
were afraid that the army would come to Beit-El and
use violence. But in the end they let me go. My father
said that usually it takes the army two to three days to
come, and it was unlikely that they could come that
night. I took my pajamas and sleeping bag and headed
for the swimming pool. I met Reut there and we
started climbing.

Halfway up the mountain we saw that my father was
wrong. A few military jeeps and police cars had already
come and soldiers were walking around talking to Ketsale and other members of the Beit-El governing council. Suddenly I got scared. Would the police really use
violence like I saw them doing on TV? How does it
happen that they use violence on the citizens of their
own nation instead of using it against the real enemy?

I was still lost in thought when my friend Michal
came up to me and told me to join the group. For
about an hour we goofed around and snacked on
sweets we had brought. Then we heard the voice of
Pinchas Wallerstein, the head of the regional council,
speaking to us through a megaphone. We crowded
around him and listened closely. This is what he said:
"Things are not going the way we expected them and
the army will be here sooner than we thought. The
army can't come up here tonight because the mountain
is too rocky and too dark, so they will probably come
tomorrow at the crack of dawn. I ask all of you, when
the soldiers come don't run away—and stay calm. We

are staying on this mountain. It is our land and if the Arabs ever come and capture the mountain it endangers all of us. Just look around—it's one of the tallest mountains in the area. You can see Beit-El and Ofra perfectly from the top. That is why we must protect this mountain with all our might, and if they take us down we will come back again and again and again.

"When the soldiers try to take you down, do not use violence under any circumstances! You may tie yourselves to rocks, to poles, to each other, and explain to them why we are doing this. But do not use violence. In the morning you will get more instructions."

Each of us went away to our own corner to get ready to go to sleep. But my friends and I didn't sleep a wink. We got up and built a campfire, then sat around and talked. At about four a.m., when the sun was starting to rise, we put out the campfire and joined a group of people who were sitting in a circle and singing Israeli and Jewish songs.

We sat down and joined the singing. At six a.m. the sun was already high in the sky, and all around on the nearby mountains was a blue mist of a clear sunny morning. We got up and made our morning prayers and ate some breakfast we had brought from home. At seven a.m. people started swarming up the mountain to strengthen us and to take part in resisting the evacuation. Now the number of women doubled and the number of men tripled. Altogether there were about 450 of us.

The evacuation was delayed and delayed. Finally, about nine a.m., we saw the soldiers climbing up the mountain. I went and sat down in the women's tent with my friends, and we hooked hands so we couldn't be moved. About two hundred troopers surrounded the men. Then the women soldiers came to us. They talked nicely and asked us to get up. Instead of getting up, we started to sing nationalistic songs. The soldiers stood around looking helpless, not knowing what to do. I felt sorry for them. They didn't want to be there and it wasn't part of their army duty. The men soldiers looked helpless too.

Then after about a half hour the Border Police came. They started barking orders at the soldiers and were upset that they were becoming too emotionally involved with the settlers.

The soldiers started pulling at the men who gripped each other even tighter. In the background I could hear Pinchas Wallerstein and Ketsale yelling and trying to keep everyone's spirits high.

Just then a woman soldier came up to me and asked me nicely to get up and go away. I didn't budge. She asked me again and I could see she was getting nervous. This time I told her that this was my land and her land too and she should come and sit with us. She said it was illegal and she had to fulfill her orders. I told her I was not getting up.

She called one of her friends and they tried to pick me up. I held on to my friends tightly, but they tugged and freed me from their grip. Then the first woman soldier held my arm tightly and led me down the mountain. Halfway down, she let go of me and said, "I'm sorry I had to do this," and turned around and marched back up.

I stood there a minute and thought about what she had said. I felt sorry for her and for all the soldiers. They didn't want to be in this position but they had orders they had to fulfill. I looked up the mountain and saw some soldiers dragging a young man about thirty years old. They looked tired and miserable. Then I knew what I would do. I pulled my small water bottle out of my pouch and went up to the soldiers. "Would you like a drink?" I asked them.

They looked at me, surprised a little, but then one of them said, "Yes, thank you," He took the bottle out of my hand and drank about half of the water and then passed it to his friend, who finished it off. They smiled at me, and then continued to carry the man down the mountain. I felt good. After all, we weren't fighting them. It wasn't their fault.

By now the sun was blazing with all its might and it was very hot. I went back up the mountain. I saw men soldiers carrying men and women soldiers carrying women. People were crying and yelling. I sat down in the tent again, and this time when a woman soldier came up to me she didn't ask me to leave. She just dragged me. I tried to resist, but she was strong and looked very strict. After about twenty feet, she pulled me to my feet and told another woman soldier to take me down. She took me all the way to the bottom this time. I saw a lot of police vans and policemen shoving men and a few women into them, probably to arrest them.

That's how it went for the rest of the day—until about four p.m. Then Pinchas Wallerstein told us to go down ourselves and not create any more problems and that he would be in negotiations with the government.

That's how it went on for a few weeks. We went up, they took us down, and we still didn't get approval from the government to build on the Artis. Then, because the government wouldn't let us build houses, we brought up two caravans and set them up as a temporary synagogue. There were prayer books and holy books in it and a couple scrolls of the Holy Torah taken from the main synagogue.

Then one day in the middle of August something terrible happened. Apparently the whole business with the mountain didn't annoy just the government. It also annoyed our Arab neighbors in Dura el-Kara, and they decided to do something about it.

They gathered a few journalists and cameramen from the world media and took them to the mountain. At the time there was only a mother and her three kids on the mountain. The Arabs climbed up the mountain from the east side yelling *Itbach el yahud!* (Slaughter the Jews) and all sorts of horrible curses against Israel, the government, and the settlers. There were about a hundred of them—men, women, and children. The Jewish mother and her three children were taken by surprise and ran to call the settlement's security officer.

The Arabs broke into the synagogue. There was a gas-powered generator there which they smashed and took the gasoline. They doused the prayer books, holy texts, and the Torah scrolls with the gasoline and burnt them. Then they burnt the generator and the Israeli flag.

In a few minutes four men arrived on the mountain in the settlement's security vehicle. They fired warning shots into the air and the Arabs started running. Two men kept firing while the other two tried to put out the fire burning the holy books.

Then one of our men shot a bullet unintentionally into the neck of an Arab. The other Arabs started screaming and quickly carried the man away. Our men put out the fire and took away the burnt and damaged books.

News about what had happened traveled fast, but it wasn't until that night that I saw the pictures on the news. It was terrible. I saw the Arabs marching up, then screaming as they set the entire mountain on fire. All you could see was a mountain with an orange top and a big cloud of smoke over it. Then I saw the men shooting in the air and taking out the Torah scroll that looked more like charcoal and ashes than our holiest book.

I couldn't stand it anymore. How much longer could the Arabs humiliate us? I broke down and cried. I was shaking all over. My father came over and hugged me. I felt angry and humiliated. It was our land, our state. Why did they think they could do anything they wanted to harm us? Why did the government let them get away with it and not care about the humiliation of the Holy Bible and G-d's name and the holy land?

The government didn't care a bit that all this happened—that the Arabs attacked a settlement. Instead they got angry that the Arab was shot, even though it was accidentally and in the defense of life. And that wasn't the worst of it. The police arrested a suspect—Mr. Ze'ev Oz, the chairman of the Beit-El governing council—and charged him with murder. The man has a wife and a family with a daughter my age. I knew hard days were coming for me and the settlement.

That night I had another dream. My friends and I

and all the people of the settlement were building new houses on the Artis. Then, like Noah, I sent away a white dove with a message in her mouth to all the land that they should come to the dedication of the new synagogue on the Artis where all the burnt Torah scrolls and holy books were restored. I waited for the dove's return, hoping it would return with an olive branch. But the dove returned with nothing. And I wondered if there would ever be peace.

Liran Zvibel

*L*iran Zvibel lives with his family in Tel Aviv, where he attends Tel Aviv University. In this story about his reactions to terrorist bombings on Purim 1996, he says that although the inability to celebrate the holiday would be sad for many Jews, the loss of the holiday to terrorism evokes a different set of emotions—particularly for the young, for whom Purim has traditionally been a light-hearted celebration.

At the same time, Zvibel is careful to say that explosions aren't always on his mind and that Israel is a wonderful place to live.

Two Awful Weeks in March

My name is Liran Zvibel. I'm sixteen years old and I live in Tel Aviv. Usually I live an ordinary life like most students my age in the world. I watch TV, study, play with my friends, talk on the phone, surf the net, etc.

Several times every year, however, our life in Israel changes. This year [1996], for example, we had several bus explosions. On the third month of the year, week

286

after week our "neighbors" made sure that our lives wouldn't be as easy and peaceful as they should be.

When the first explosion happened in Jerusalem all the students and teachers of my grade gathered together into one very big room and discussed the situation—how everyone was afraid and that our country isn't safe anymore. All who had something to say were free to say it and everybody supported them. Later we sang some sad songs and showed the pictures of the innocent dead people.

Two or three days later another explosion happened in Jerusalem and we did the same things. We all were even more upset and most of us cried. I especially remember something one of the students said. In Israel every person who dies is pictured on the cover of the morning papers. The students pointed out that after every explosion the pictures of the dead become smaller since there are more dead and the paper doesn't get any bigger. The wounded's pictures don't even make it to the front page. At a time like that, nobody smiled.

In days like these it is very hard for the students to learn and even harder for the teachers to teach. A teaching job in Israel is much harder than in a normal country since the teachers have to deal with some very serious problems. An example was when the third explosion happened during Chag Purim, a week after the first one. "Chag" in Hebrew means a special holiday. All the kids (and some of the adults too) dress up like funny things. Some people work months on their costumes, and every year there is a great festival. Since people worked for months we decided to go ahead and have the festival at school but not to make it too noisy and happy.

On the morning of the school celebration of Chag Purim I turned on the radio to hear the morning news, and I heard that there was another explosion. I was already dressed up—like a woman, actually. If I hadn't had the hair on my legs, I could have been a very convincing woman. I didn't know what to do. I didn't know whether to go dressed as I was or to change to regular clothes, and my parents didn't know what to tell me either. I called my teacher. I didn't wake her up because another student had already done it. After a little conversation she told me to bring my costume in a plastic bag and to see what the other students did.

I missed my bus because of having to undress and my father drove me to school. In the car I thought it over and came to the conclusion that teachers in Israel have a very hard job—they have to make too difficult decisions.

We were listening to the car radio and the reporter repeated the news from earlier, but this time he said, "For those who just woke up—this isn't a tape. There was another bus explosion THIS MORNING." This was a horrible line.

When I got to school there were some students who came dressed up. One said she didn't want to take her clothes off since it took her a lot of time to put them on and that if she had taken her clothes off she would probably have been late for school. The others didn't hear the bad news and felt bad about being dressed up. The festival, as you might have guessed, didn't take place. Every year the tenth graders are the ones who are in charge of the festival. They worked on it for more than four months and now they couldn't show what they had prepared. We couldn't concentrate on our lessons and so we just talked with each other and with our teachers.

We supported each other and were supported by the teachers. These kinds of tragic situations help to make the relationship between the students and the teachers much closer— even intimate sometimes.

Later that day there was an explosion by Disingof Center—a huge mall in Disingof Street. It was close to 4:00 P.M. and there were a lot of people there. The upper floors are offices and my father works in one of those offices. The explosion was under my father's office. Disingof Center, like most malls, has a lot of glass in it and the explosion destroyed most of it, so there were many wounded and dead. Our luck was that my father called us and told us about the explosion before it was on the radio or on the TV so that we wouldn't be worried. The only problem was that my father couldn't get home since the main road was destroyed by the bomb and the other roads were closed by the police.

About a year before there had been another explosion in Disingof. This explosion is known as "the bus number 5 explosion." My math teacher came and told us that something terrible happened in Disingof Street but tried to keep on teaching. Both of my parents work on Disingof Street and I didn't have any information about the situation. I had no way to contact my parents. When I got home I was so relieved to find them both at home.

*   *   *

In this story I told you about a very little part of my life as a teenager growing up in Israel. You might think that we don't live a regular life and are afraid all the time. Well, this is not true! I don't feel fear at all—at least not about explosions. Like most of the teenagers in the world I live my life in peace and don't even think of explosions. Israel is a great place to live in. We have a great climate, gorgeous people, and beautiful beaches. I remember walking in Washington D.C. after dark, and I think that then I was afraid! I saw all the poor homeless who were asking for money, and I ran to my hotel! In this aspect Israel is much safer than the United States.

The only problem is that we have some enemies around us and unless we have peace with them we won't be able to live in true peace with ourselves. I don't say that because I belong to the left wing. As a matter of fact, I belong to the right wing.

I don't know how well you get the whole picture. Wherever you live, I just want you to know that there is NOBODY in Israel who doesn't want peace. The problem is that many of us have different ideas for how this peace should be gotten and how much we should sacrifice for it.

Credits

The Holocaust and World War II

Berg, Mary (pseudonym). *Warsaw Ghetto: A Diary.* S. L. Shneiderman, ed. Prepared by Norbert Guterman and Sylvia Glass, New York: L. B. Fischer Publishing Corporation, 1945.

Heshele, Janina. "Excerpts from Janina Heshele's Diary of Lvov." Translated and edited by Azriel Eisenberg from Hebrew translation of original Polish edition. This excerpt appeared in *The Lost Generation: Children in the Holocaust,* New York: Pilgrim Press, 1982. (The excerpt in Hebrew that Azriel Eisenberg used to make his translation into English was in the following book: Bartura, Abraham. *Hayelad Vehonoar Bashoa Ugvurah (Children and Youth in the Holocaust and Resistance).* Israel: Kiryat Sefer, 1965. I have been unable to locate any reference to the title or whereabouts of the original Polish edition, which may have been only privately published.)

Kinsky-Pollack, Helga. "Excerpts from the Terezín Diary of Twelve-Year-Old Helga Kinsky of Vienna." In *Terezín.* Frantisek Ehrmann, Otta Heitlinger, and Rudolf Iltis, eds. Prague: Council of Jewish Communities in the Czech Lands, 1965, pp. 103–05.

Konstantinova, Ina. "Diary and Letters." In *Defending Leningrad: Women Behind Enemy Lines.* © by Kazimiera J. Cottam, Ph.D., editor and translator. Nepean, Ontario: New Military Publishing, 1998. Distributed by Vanwell Publishing Limited. P.O. Box 2131, 1 Northrup Crescent, St. Catharines, ON L2R 7S2, Canada. Originally published in Russian: *Devushka iz Kashina.* Molodaya gvardiya (the publishing house of the Young Communist League), 1947. Latest Soviet edition: *Devushka iz Kashina: Dnevnik i pis'ma I. Konstantinovoy, vospominaniya i ocherki o ney. [The Girl from Kashin: The Diary and Letters of I. Konstantinova, Reminiscences and Sketches Concerning Her.]* Moscow: Moskovskiy Rabochiy Publishing House, 1974.

Perry, Colin. *Boy in the Blitz.* Originally published in Great Britain by Leo Cooper Limited, 1972. (Copyright Colin Perry, 1972.) Corgi edition published in 1974. Colin A. Perry Limited Edition published in 1980.

Phillips, Janine. *My Secret Diary*. London: Shepheard-Walwyn (Publishers) Ltd., 1982. German edition: *Polen, Mai 1939: Ein Tagebuch*. Ravensburg: O. Maier, 1982.

Van der Heide, Dirk (pseudonym). Translated by Mrs. Antoon Deventer. *My Sister and I*. New York: Harcourt, Brace, and Co., Inc., 1941.

"The Troubles" in Northern Ireland

"Neil," © Lisa Burrows, Moy, County Tyrone, Northern Ireland, 1995.

"The Leaving of Liverpool," © Kevin Byers, Portaferry, County Down, Northern Ireland, 1995.

"The Road Rats Cometh," © Stephen Hoey, Enniskillen, County Fermanagh, Northern Ireland, 1995.

"Eamon," © John McConnell, Belfast, Northern Ireland, 1995.

"Internment," © Margaret McCrory, Cookstown, County Tyrone, Northern Ireland, 1995.

"Condemned," © Brenda Murphy, Belfast, Northern Ireland, 1995.

"Unwelcome Callers," © Alison Östnas, Bangor, County Down, Northern Ireland, 1995.

"Clutch of Fear," © P. J. Quinn, Belfast, Northern Ireland, 1995.

"Kneecapped," © Margaret E. Simpson, Belfast, Northern Ireland, 1995.

The Israeli/Palestinian Conflict

"Marked For Destruction," © Ibtisam S. Barakat, Columbia, Missouri, U.S.A., 1998.

"Going to Jerusalem," © Gunter David, Ft. Washington, Pennsylvania, U.S.A., 1998.

"A Look into Memory," © Ghareeb (pseud.), Ramallah, West Bank, via Israel, 1998.

"Alti Zachen," © Victoria Kay-Feinerman, Petach Tikva, Israel, 1998.

"Face of Peace," © Redrose (pseud.), Rishon Le Tzion, Israel, 1998.

"Born in Bethlehem," © Marina Riadi, Atlanta, Georgia, U.S.A., 1998.

"A Christian Palestinian's Story," © Wadad Saba, Seattle, Washington, U.S.A., 1998.

"My Life on the Firing Line," © Racheli Tal, Beit-El, Israel, 1998.

"Two Awful Weeks in March," © Liran Zvibel, Tel Aviv, Israel, 1998.

About the Author

LAUREL HOLLIDAY, formerly a college teacher, editor, and psychotherapist, now writes full time in Seattle. She is the award-winning author of *Children in the Holocaust and World War II: Their Secret Diaries; Children of "The Troubles": Our Lives in the Crossfire of Northern Ireland;* and *Children of Israel, Children of Palestine: Our Own True Stories,* all published by Pocket Books. Her most recent book is *Children of the Dream: Our Own Stories of Growing Up Black in America* (also published by Pocket Books).

Bullying.
Threats.
Bullets.

Locker
searches?
Metal
detectors?

Fight back without fists.

fight for your rights:
take a stand against violence

WARRIORS DON'T CRY

A TRUE STORY YOU WON'T FORGET

Melba Pattillo Beals

The dramatic true story of the battle to integrate Little Rock's Central High

"I was only fifteen, and I was afraid for my life. But our dreams were stronger than their hatred."

By the winner of the Congressional Gold Medal

Including 8 pages of photographs

Now available from Archway Paperbacks

Published by Pocket Books